Mastering Machine Appliqué

BY HARRIET HARGRAVE

2nd Edition

THE COMPLETE GUIDE INCLUDING

- ♥ Invisible Machine Appliqué
- ♥ Satin Stitch
- ♥ Blanket Stitch & Much More

C&T PUBLISHING

© 2001 Harriet Hargrave

Editor: Jan Grigsby
Technical Editor: Carolyn Aune
Copy Editor: Lucy Grijalva
Design Director/Book Design: Christina D. Jarumay
Cover Design: Christina D. Jarumay
Production Assistant: Tim Manibusan
Graphic Illustrations: Richard Sheppard
Cover Image: Currants and Coxcomb block, Harriet Hargrave
Photography: Brian Birlauf

Attention Teachers:
C&T Publishing, Inc. encourages you to use this book as a text for teaching. Contact us at 800-284-1114 or www.ctpub.com for more information about the C&T Teachers Program.

Library of Congress Cataloging-in-Publication Data
Hargrave, Harriet.
  Mastering machine appliqué : the complete guide including invisible machine appliqué, satin stitch, blanket stitch & much more / by Harriet Hargrave.-- 2nd ed.
      p. cm.
Rev. ed. of: Mastering machine appliqué, the satin stitch. c1991
Includes index.
  ISBN 1-57120-136-X
  1. Machine appliqué. I. Hargrave, Harriet. Mastering machine appliqué, the satin stitch. II. Title.
  TT779 .H35 2001
  746.46--dc21
                          2001005217

Published by C&T Publishing, Inc.
P.O. Box 1456
Lafayette, California 94549

Printed in China
10 9 8 7 6 5 4 3 2 1

Dedication

The first edition of this book was dedicated to my daughter Carrie, for her sacrifices that allowed me to pursue my dreams and goals. I stated then that I hoped I had given her the permission to follow her dreams, and I am proud to state that she has. Her association with quilters has kept her down to earth and her worldwide travels with me have opened up the world for her to explore. This edition is also dedicated to her, as she has learned to follow her heart instead of pursuing money, and she is well on her way to a successful and fulfilling life. Also because appliqué is her favorite technique in the art of quiltmaking.

Table of

Contents

Introduction

Machine appliqué does not have a long, romantic history of genteel ladies' works of art. Instead, most popular forms of machine applique have been in existence only since the development of the zigzag sewing machine (many of the techniques in this book have been developed within the last 20 years). The popularity of machine appliqué has not been constant, and the quality has had a tendency to be moderate until the past few years.

I began my machine appliqué career in the late 1970s, when I made loads of items to sell at art and craft shows. I specialized in the infamous 'hoop pictures' and baby quilts. My products were the platform by which I started teaching adult education in 1978, then on to opening my quilt store in 1980. I have always been a stickler for high-quality supplies and equipment, and using the appropriate product for the job to be done. I have taught this way for the past 22 years, and many students have achieved great success following the guidelines I present in my classrooms. I cannot stress enough how important attention to detail and PRACTICING are to high quality workmanship.

The first edition of *Mastering Machine Appliqué* has been a long time standard for obtaining high-quality stitching. However, after using the book for 10 years in the classroom, I find that many technical points were not covered with enough depth, and some of the products and techniques needed updating. Therefore, I am rewriting and updating the book, making it more of a workbook.

When using this book, I strongly suggest that you first read it entirely, getting a good idea of the techniques possible and the supplies that you will need to collect. Then go through it again, only with the idea of practicing and learning the techniques in mind. Please do not practice on a project that you have great hopes for!! Nothing is more frustrating than wanting a project to turn out really well, only to find that you don't have the skill level to pull it off. I constantly advise my students to slow down, take a breath, and remember what it was like as a child to learn a new skill.

A study at John Hopkins University found that it takes six hours to permanently store any new physical skill into your memory. If the storage process is interrupted by learning another new skill, the first lesson may be erased. The study showed that time itself is a very powerful component of learning; it is not enough to simply practice something, you have to allow time for the brain to encode the new skill. What this means to you is that you have to practice, think about the skill, repeat it over time, then you will 'have' it. Today, we seem to think that if we do it once, we should be able to do it well—automatically. This is not how our brain works.

Sample Books

I strongly advise you to make sample books that contain pages of your practice samples. On these samples, note what you have discovered as you develop each skill, such as tension settings for your machine, threads of preference, stitch width and length settings, etc. Learn the stitching techniques first—really well—then when you start your projects, the finished results will be something you are proud of. If you make the project first, it is too often the case that because you are disappointed in the final result, you will not attempt the technique again, thinking, "I can't do that". Practice is the only way you will become proficient at any skill.

The samples you are about to make are great notebook samples. I can't stress enough how invaluable notebooks of stitch samples are;

they eliminate the need to re-test your machine over and over. I use 5" x 9" 3-ring notebooks with sheet protectors. The sample fabric is cut to size and backed with a stabilizer. Freezer paper will do for your samples. Make notes, indicate tension settings, stitch width and length settings, etc. on the fabric beside the stitches you make. As you experiment with different widths, lengths, threads, tension settings, and needles, you will have a permanent record of your experiments. Once this is done, you not only know how to control the machine and make the stitches look the way you want them to, but you have a reference manual to revisit time and again, with all the settings recorded for future use.

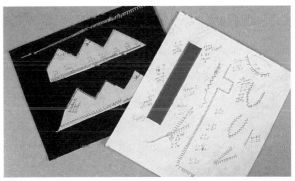

Samples

Enough of my soapbox. You can tell that I have taught for a long time! I sincerely hope you enjoy the process of mastering the machine appliqué techniques presented here, and that you succeed in many years of producing stunning quilts and projects.

Have fun!

CHAPTER 1

Equipment

Machine appliqué requires specific equipment and supplies to obtain professional-looking results. You may already have many of these; others will be new products that you may not know about. Read through the Equipment and Supplies chapters before starting any projects. Then you can assemble everything you need before you begin to practice, with a thorough understanding of the items and their use.

Sewing Machines

You must have a zigzag for machine appliqué. Whereas most machines provide the stitches required for appliqué, a machine that works with you, not against you, definitely enhances the quality of your work. Tension control, stitch width and length control, the proper feet, stitch quality and the capability to adjust to many different applications and threads are all critical. When considering the machine you will use to learn these appliqué techniques, or if you are interested in buying a new or different machine, you may find the following list useful.

Suggested machine features:

❋ Perfect tension, regardless of what combination of thread is put into the machine.

❋ The capability to adjust the bobbin tension (with the bobbin case itself or by purchasing a separate bobbin case).

❋ Up-and-down needle position on command. Some machines provide this feature in the foot control, giving the user control of every half stitch. Others have an electronic button that keeps the needle either up or down all the time.

❋ Complete adjustability of stitch width. You will appreciate having the ability to make the stitch any size you need it to be; not what the machine predetermines is correct. Digital machines often have .5 between stitch width sizes, for example: 2 – 2.5 – 3.0 – 3.5 etc. This hinders your ability to totally control the finished look of the stitch. Check this feature on your machine before starting, and definitely check it when shopping for new equipment. The ultimate machine has unlimited stitch width settings on a dial that can be very finely adjusted while sewing.

✳ The capability to make the stitch length very small is a must. Make sure that the satin stitch on the machine provides complete coverage —there should be no gaps between the stitches.

✳ Adjustable needle positions.

✳ The capability to override any pre-set computer settings.

✳ The capability to sew for hours at high speed without overheating.

✳ A reputable dealer who will help with minor adjustments and have an understanding of what you are doing.

Stitches

When Satin stitching, your machine needs to have the capability to adjust both stitch width and stitch length while you sew.

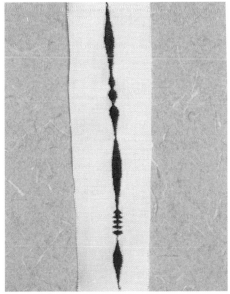

Satin stitch with width adjustments

Most of today's machines are digital, with push buttons to adjust the width. The most desirable feature on a machine for appliqué is a dial that allows the stitch to be made any width you desire, and with the ability

to taper the width down to the sharpest point. A push button machine generally increases and decreases in increments of .5mm, which causes a slight stair-stepping action. The more increments given with a push of the button, the more control you have of the stitch; machines that offer increments of .1mm or .2mm are preferable.

For Invisible Machine appliqué techniques, you need a straight Blind stitch.

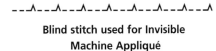

Blind stitch used for Invisible Machine Appliqué

When setting the machine up for Invisible Machine appliqué, the ability to make the stitch width and length very small is a must. The stitch width is so narrow that it will catch only 2 threads of the edge of the appliqué—about 0.5mm. Many machines will not allow the user to go narrower than 2mm wide. If this is the case on your machine, check to see if you have a double needle override. This feature is on many Pfaff® models and will allow you to make very narrow stitches. The stitch length needed is no more than 1/8".

Blanket stitching also requires that the machine be fully adjustable in stitch width and length, and that the stitch is a true Blanket stitch.

Blanket stitch

Many Blanket stitches go forward and backward a few times, or take little stitches between each zigzag, or even within the zigzag stitch, which all detract from the look we desire. As a general rule, mechanical machines do not have a Blanket stitch. It is a feature more commonly found on computerized machines.

♥ **Instructions given in this book are for machines that have a center needle position during basic sewing functions. Machines with a permanent left-hand needle position make it very difficult to accomplish many of these techniques.**

Presser Feet

An open-toe or appliqué foot will make all appliqué techniques easier. It should not have a metal or plastic bar between the toes in front of the needle, that can block your view of each stitch as it is being made. On the bottom of the foot, there should be a long, deep groove running the center length of the foot. Ideally, this groove is flanged to allow for turning of corners and tight curves.

Tip *You can often adapt your embroidery or decorative stitch foot by cutting out the center piece of metal or plastic, and filing it smooth, so that you can see clearly.*

Bottom

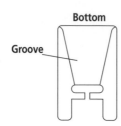
Bottom

Groove

Presser foot with flat bottom **Presser foot with grooved bottom**

This groove allows the height of the Satin stitch to pass freely under the foot without jamming. Without the groove, the foot catches on the mound of thread, and the fabric cannot feed forward smoothly.

If an open-toe or appliqué foot is not available from the machine manufacturer, you can often purchase a "generic" foot that will fit. This foot is sometimes referred to as a "buttonhole" foot as well.

The open-toe or appliqué foot is used for most of the techniques presented in this book. When Straight stitch techniques are used, you may find it helpful to use an edge-stitching foot. This resembles the blind hem foot but does not have the bar that the stitch crosses to add ease in the stitch. The edge-stitching foot is simply used to help you sew more accurately.

Most importantly, your vision should not be hindered by anything in front of the needle when doing the very close work of these techniques; you must be able to see every stitch as it is being made.

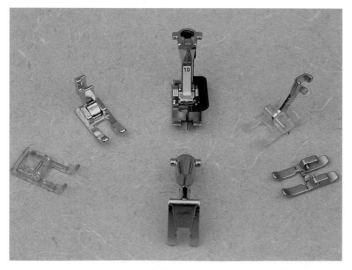

Open-toe, appliqué, and edge-stitching feet for different machine types

Sewing Machine Needles

Needles are critical in obtaining a smooth, even stitch when Satin stitching. You want a tiny, invisible stitch while Invisible Machine appliquéing, and a heavy, hand-stitch look when doing Blanket stitching. You will find that your choice of needle will definitely affect the final look of your project. When Satin stitching, the extreme density of the stitches tends to dull and heat a needle, so you will need to change the needle more often than when doing normal sewing. Too large a needle allows the stitches to be visible when trying to Invisible Machine appliqué. Heavier threads are used in Blanket stitching techniques, requiring a heavier needle, often with a larger eye.

Use only high-quality machine needles, and start each new project with a new needle. Check your manual for the size, type, and brand of needle recommended for your machine to prevent poor quality and/or skipped stitches. This information is sometimes found imprinted in the bobbin area of the machine, or within your owner's manual.

Tip *There is no guarantee that all the needles in a new package are in perfect condition. You might run across a damaged needle, even though it has never been used. If you are having problems with the stitch quality, don't overlook the needle as a possible culprit, even though you just changed it to a new one.*

Below are illustrations of a needle and the terms used to describe it.

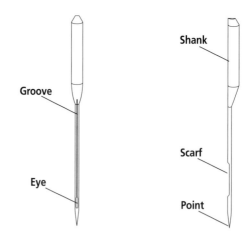

Shank

Groove

Scarf

Eye

Point

The needle is flat on one side of the shank, and has a long groove on the opposite side. The groove allows the thread to be protected within the needle while penetrating the material. The other side will hold the thread as it goes through the material. The thread slides through the grooved side and the eye, and because it is pinched from behind, it creates a loop behind the needle as the needle rises. This loop and the scarf (the hollowed out area on the back of the needle) allow the hook point of the shuttle to pass between the thread and the needle, locking the stitch.

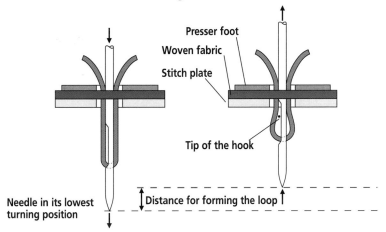

Thread loop being formed as needle leaves fabric

Needle sizes are determined by measuring the width of the needle blade. The European system is widely accepted, but for reference, the U.S. equivalents are shown below.

Needle Size Equivalents

	Lightweight fabrics			Medium-weight fabrics				Heavyweight fabrics	
European	60	65	70	75	80	90	100	110	120
U.S.	8	9	10	11	12	14	16	18	20

The information that you need is printed on the front of the needle packet. There are two important sets of numbers on it.

❋ The first number to look for is the system number, which is stated as 15 x 1, or 705B, or 705H. This is the number that determines which needle is suitable for your particular machine. Check your sewing machine manual to find out what needle system is correct for your particular machine.

❋ The second important number on the needle packet is the needle size. This number indicates the thickness of the blade of the needle, which determines its suitability for a given fabric. Most needle packets have both the metric and U.S. sizes.

❋ In addition, you will often find an additional letter or set of letters behind the system number, such as S for stretch, L for leather, M for microtex sharp.

Schmetz® generally writes the type of needle it is when it is a specialty needle, such as embroidery or quilting.

❋ Needles may have a colored shank to identify them once they are out of the package.

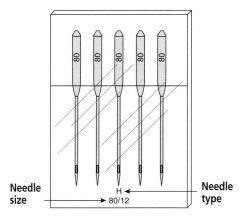

Tip The top of the Schmetz needle packet is magnified, making the needle sizes imprinted on the needle shank easier to read.

There are many sizes and varieties of needles. Long ago when there were only natural-fiber fabrics all needles had sharp points, so we purchased needles by size only. As we know more about fabrics and have developed so many specialty needles, we have learned that we get the best quality stitch with the smallest possible needle, with the appropriate point, for any given project. When selecting a needle, consider the overall shape, its application, and the thread that is going to go through it.

Needle sizes

The following list is a general guide-line for needle size choices. Don't forget that the eye of the needle is directly proportional to its circumference. Be sure to read the thread section in Chapter Two, as well as refer to the chart below to identify which weight thread is best used with each of these needles.

60/8 – This needle is best for very lightweight fabrics such as chiffon. Excellent for Invisible Machine appliqué when stitching through a single thickness of fabric.

65/9 – These are fairly new. Best used with tightly woven, silk-like fabrics (rayon, polyester) as well as real silk. This is the smallest needle you can use with standard weight thread if fine thread is not available.

70/10 – Used for average light-to-medium-weight woven fabrics such as shirtings, batiste, cotton lawns. Excellent for machine embroidery and appliqué when used with fine threads.

80/12 – This is the most flexible size needle for use in both cotton wovens and knits in the mid-range of density.

90/14 – This larger needle is used with denim, jeans, corduroy, and decorator—weight fabrics.

100/16 – Used for backed upholstery and very heavy and dense fabrics like fake furs.

110/18 – Anytime you use a needle larger than 100/16, you are purposely creating a hole. Use this needle (and larger) for hemstitching and decorative work. A wing needle is designed specifically to create a hole.

> *Tip* *If the needle is thicker than the density of the fabric it must go through, it will break. Don't think that a larger needle won't break on thick fabrics. And—too big a needle used on a piece of heavy fabric can ruin the timing on your machine.*

Needle types

Now, let's walk through the various types of needles available today, using the Schmetz brand for reference. These are some of the highest quality needles made; Schmetz has developed a needle for our every need. Most sewing machine manufacturers recommend Schmetz needles for best results.

As you go through the following list of needles, remember there are always exceptions. For instance, you might find that your machine performs best on a certain technique with a needle that is not meant for that application.

Needle/Thread Reference								
Thread Size					**Needle Size**			
	60	**65**	**70**	**75**	**80**	**90**	**100**	**110**
Ultra fine 80/2	•	•						
Nylon monofilament	•	•	•	•	•			
Fine machine embroidery 60/2		•	•	•				
DMC® machine embroidery thread 50/2		•	•	•				
Embroidery thread 30/2			•	•	•			
Merc. cotton sewing thread 50/3				•	•			
Synthetic sewing thread (spun)				•	•			
Cotton-wrapped polyester						•		
Cotton 40/3						•	•	
Buttonhole (cordonnet)							•	•

> *Tip* *The best rule of thumb is: If in doubt, make a test seam or stitching sample using the fabric, needle, and thread you will use in your project. Start with the needle that seems the most appropriate and fine-tune from there within sizes and types.*

Almost all sewing machine needles have a round point. The choice of the most suitable round point depends on the properties of the fabric to be sewn and whether that fabric is natural or synthetic. Round-point needles do not pierce the threads of the material, but are turned aside by them into the gaps between the threads. The coarser the fabric thread, the more the point must be rounded. Most fabrics can be sewn satisfactorily with needles having a slightly rounded point, better known as the Universal point needle.

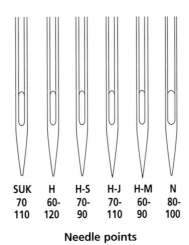

Needle points

SUK	H	H-S	H-J	H-M	N
70-110	60-120	70-90	70-110	60-90	80-100

SUK, SKL or SKF These are true ballpoint needles—they are used on fabrics with Spandex®, some elastics and coarse knitwear. Elastic materials with rubber or elastic threads require needles with special or heavy ballpoints. These points also push the threads aside without perforating them. When sewing difficult projects and materials, experiment with various needle sizes and points to see which one achieves the best stitch quality. Available in sizes 70/10 – 110/18.

H The Schmetz H series denotes a point or shape that is neither strictly sharp nor ballpoint. It is an all-purpose needle point for most knits and wovens. It is barely rounded at the tip and has a scarf. The 80/12-H is the needle used most for general sewing and piecing; it is known as the Universal needle. Available in sizes 60/8–120/20.

H-S The S needle was developed for fabrics that are susceptible to damage – such as highly stretchable synthetic knitted material and synthetic suedes. The S stands for stretch.

It has a less rounded point than ballpoint needles, and prevents skipped stitches in these fabrics. Available in sizes 70/10–90/14.

H-J When we saw natural fibers, especially denim, return in popularity some years ago, the needle manufacturers were forced back to the drawing board. They had to re-introduce sharp needles that were capable of penetrating tightly woven, dense fibers. The J stands for jeans. When sewing a tight or coarsely woven fabric with a ballpoint needle, a slight zigzag appearance may result as the needle deflects off the threads instead of piercing them. The acute round point of the 705HJ needle, also known as a jeans needle, has a sharper point which pierces the threads of the fabric, resulting in a uniform, straight stitch. This needle is designed to be used on woven fabrics. Available in sizes 70/10 –110/18.

H-Q The Q stands for quilting. This needle is designed with a special taper to the point in order to prevent damage to quilting fabrics, as well as gliding in and out of thick seam allowances faster and easier, preventing broken needles and skipped stitches. Available in sizes 75/11 and 90/14.

H-E The embroidery needle has a larger eye to accommodate heavier embroidery threads. The scarf is designed to help reduce skipped stitches and the thread groove is deeper to protect delicate threads like rayon from shredding. Available in sizes 75/11 and 90/14.

H-M The M stands for microtex, otherwise known as a sharp needle. This needle has the sharpest point of all sewing machine needles available. It provides perfectly straight stitches —ideal for fine cottons and silks, topstitching, and edge stitching. Available in sizes 60/8–90/14.

130/MET Known as Metallica®, as well as the Metalfil® (by Sullivan); is used when stitching with metallic threads. It has a unique finish that helps control heat, as well as a specialized eye and scarf that help eliminate the stripping and splitting so common with metallic threads. Available in sizes 80/12 and 90/14.

130N This needle series is for topstitching. The eye is double the size of the Universal needle to accommodate heavy threads. Available in sizes 80/12–100/16.

On the following page is a reference chart of various types of needles and their general uses, as well as needle/thread compatibility. Remember that machine needles vary according to the type of point and the thickness of the needle. Needles are selected for the type and weight of fabric being sewn, as well as the thread you are sewing with. The list above demonstrates that there is a lot to the science of machine needles; to get the best performance from your machine, your understanding of the differences between types is very important.

Suggested Uses for Various Needle Types

Fabric	Needle Size	Point Code
Quilting weight cottons	75/11	H-J for piecing
	80/12	H-Q for quilting
		H- for piecing & quilting
Heavier cottons	80/12	H-J for piecing
Flannels	90/14	H-Q for quilting
Silks, satins, delicate fabrics	70/10	H-M for piecing
Any fabric where you are using metallic or heavy machine embroidery threads	80/12	H-MET
	90/14	H-MET
Any fabric where you are using rayon threads	75/11	H-E
	90/14	H-E

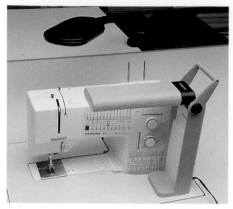

OTT light set up around sewing machine

Work Space

Appliqué can cause a great deal of eye and neck strain. It is very close work, so a good workstation with adequate light is very necessary. Consider the following when setting up a space for you to perform appliqué techniques comfortably, and to learn more about setting up a sewing workspace see Chapter 3 in *The Art of Classic Quiltmaking.*

Lighting

I cannot stress too strongly the importance of adequate lighting in your workspace. Without it, you risk constant eye fatigue. Overall good lighting in the room is a start, but appliqué requires concentrated lighting at the sewing machine.

The wattage of the sewing machine light is only 15 watts. If the machine light was any brighter, it would also be hotter, causing problems for the machine's circuitry, but this is not enough light to see the detail involved in appliqué. The addition of good lighting around the needle is critical.

I personally prefer to sew by OTT® lights. I have the small portable one in front of the needle, and the Flex Arm unit behind the machine. These lights give true-color, full-spectrum light that is very easy on the eyes. The gooseneck lights that so many of us use create glare and reflection that is hard on the eyes. If you haven't tried an OTT light yet, try one and you will certainly see the difference.

Light Box

A light box is not an absolute necessity, but it is a true asset when tracing or positioning pattern pieces onto another layer of fabric. It enables you to see paper patterns through fabrics, eliminating the step of tracing placement lines onto the fabric itself. Traced lines tend to be inaccurate, showing outside the edge of the appliqué piece, and hard to remove.

Often quite expensive if purchased from an art supply store, a light box can be made at home by simply placing a sheet of glass over the leaf opening of your dining room table and using a bare light bulb in a lamp on the floor underneath the glass. Your sewing machine cabinet can also be utilized. Take the machine out of the cabinet, and lay a fluorescent light like the OTT light on the platform that the machine generally sits on. Have a piece of acrylic cut to fit the opening and use it instead of the machine insert. You now have a great working surface that is multi-task.

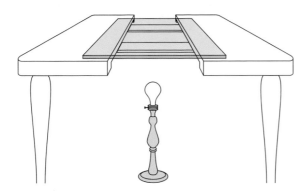

Making a light box with dining room table

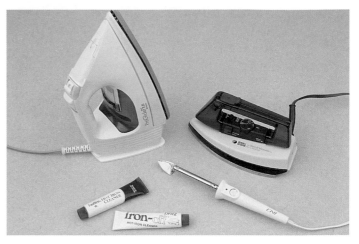

Irons and iron cleaners

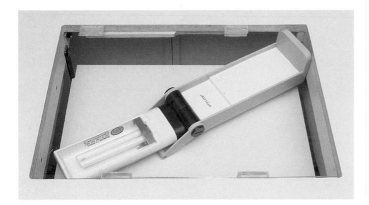

OTT light in sewing machine cabinet for light box

You could also build a wooden box and add kitchen under-counter fluorescent light sticks and a sheet of acrylic to create a portable light box. You can adapt a child's Lite-Brite® toy if you have one, or a window is the old-fashioned standby.

Irons

A full-size iron is preferable when working on larger pieces and a small travel iron with a sharp point is ideal for small work. The new Clover Mini Iron® is especially nice when working with small seam allowances and/or shapes. If you have an old dry iron, use it as your appliqué iron. Its smooth surface provides more even heat distribution than a steam iron, which has holes in the sole plate. If using an older iron make sure that it still heats up sufficiently to bond fusibles.

The bottom of your iron needs to be kept clean and smooth, free of any residue from sizing and finishes from fabrics, as well as residue from fusibles. There are commercial iron cleaners that are available at your local quilt or fabric store. Many of the newer irons have sole plates that will not scratch and that fusibles cannot stick to, making them problem-free when working with fusing agents.

A large piece of muslin or a non-stick pressing sheet (see Chapter Two) covering your ironing board will protect it from residue from fusibles, so that they won't damage garments ironed later.

Photocopy Machine

Having a small, desktop photocopy machine available is a real time-saver. You can use it to copy multiple pattern pieces onto freezer paper and to copy directly onto fabric. The machine needs to have the ability to enlarge and reduce, and it needs a manual feeding system as well as a tray feed. Details on these ideas are in Chapter Twenty.

CHAPTER 2

Supplies

Many things affect the appliqué process. Threads, needles, stabilizers, and fabrics all play an important role in how easily you accomplish the task and how successful your finished project is.

Your knowledge and understanding of thread greatly impacts the quality of your appliqué work. My students are always amazed at the difference a simple thing like changing to the correct needle and the correct thread size and type make on the outcome of the finished product. Be very particular when choosing the size, brand, and quality of the thread you plan to use in your machine appliqué techniques. High-quality thread is essential to fine stitch quality.

Threads

Different types of embroidery threads

I strongly suggest that you learn the techniques in this book using 100% cotton machine embroidery threads. Cotton threads are softer than man-made fibers and tend to untwist and spread a little on the surface, giving much better coverage without crowding the stitches. Cotton is also a more flexible fiber than polyester. This flexibility produces a smoother, more consistent Satin stitch. Cotton thread also has a much lower thread drag than synthetic threads, allowing your machine tensions to create a nicer looking stitch.

When buying thread, we too often select according to color, not paying enough attention to the size or ply of the thread. These two factors are often a mystery to us. The numbers on the spool may or may not mean anything to you, such as 30, 40/3, 60/2, etc. These numbers tell us the thickness of the thread and the number of plies. The higher the number, the finer the thread is. The number behind the slash indicates how many plies are twisted together. This system can be used to determine how fine the thread is and for what purposes it can be used.

Machine embroidery threads are 2-ply threads. They are loosely twisted, very weak and soft, and allow the stitches to build up and fill in tightly in the stitching process, without jamming. Purchase only machine embroidery threads when Satin stitching or performing any other decorative work done on the machine where there is a buildup of stitches. Sewing threads are too bulky, too tightly twisted, and stitch unevenly and/or jam in these situations.

Thread sizes on their spools

Several brands and sizes of machine embroidery thread are available; these are made of long-fiber cotton, which reduces snagging and breaking. They also have a consistency of diameter resulting in uniformity of stitches and less thread drag than other brands. DMC makes size 50/2 thread. Swiss/Metrosene makes Mettler® embroidery thread in size 30/2 (yellow printing on the spool) and size 60/2 (green printing on the spool). The larger the number, the thinner the thread. I highly recommend using the 50/2 DMC or the 60/2 Mettler for Satin stitching. The 30/2 is an excellent Blanket stitching thread. It is twice as heavy as 50 or 60, and fills in the stitch with a heavier look. Refer to the chart on page 19 for uses of each thread and the appropriate needle for each.

When Satin or Blanket stitching, remember that the color of the thread and the width of the stitch can affect the overall appearance of the piece. When choosing your thread color, consider that a slightly darker thread will frame a piece best and cover more completely. A lighter color will make the design seem to shine on the edges.

I strongly recommend using only size 60/2 in the bobbin when working with cotton embroidery threads in the needle. When used in the bobbin, this very thin thread reduces excessive buildup in the stitch. White, black, and medium gray are the most used bobbin colors, but if there are tension problems, matching the bobbin thread to the top thread or fabric color may be necessary. If both sides of the project will be seen, definitely match top and bottom threads. Size 80/2 thread is also available, and is an excellent choice for bobbin thread.

When working with rayon or metallic embroidery threads, Bobbinfil® and Sew Bob® are good choices. These are nylon lingerie threads and work nicely with synthetic threads in the needle.

> *Tip* *Basting cotton is often sold for bobbin thread for machine artwork, but I do not recommend it. It is a very short-fiber thread (which creates a lot of lint in the machine), its diameter is irregular, and the thickness of the thread causes excessive buildup. Mettler fine embroidery, 60 weight/2-ply is far superior. Pre-wound bobbins are most often synthetic thread. I suggest you wind your own with the recommended thread.*

Size .004 invisible monofilament quilting thread is used for Invisible Machine appliqué. This is a very soft nylon that allows your machine Blind stitch to look just like a hand-stitched edge. It is used only on the top to prevent breakage and jamming. Be very particular when purchasing this thread; if it is too weak or too strong, it will give unsatisfactory results. Buy it on small cones in 1,000- to 1,500-yard quantities. Anything larger than this will age poorly and become brittle before it can be used. My personal favorite is Sew Art International Invisible® thread. It is the thread I use for my quilting and Invisible machine appliqué, and I have had superior results to all others on the market. It does not shine on the surface of the quilt, and seems to glide through the machine more smoothly than any other thread available today. Wonder Thread® from YLI (Yarn Loft International) would be my second choice if Sew Art were not available. Be aware that Wonder Thread does shine, and many machines do not sew with it as easily as Sew Art. Look for the label on the bottom of the cone.

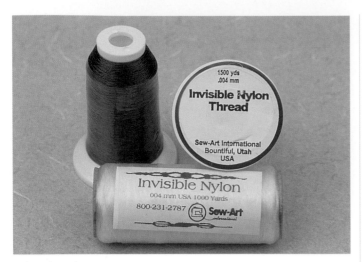

Nylon thread

As you develop your skills in machine appliqué, you will probably be tempted to try various other threads for effect. Rayon and metallic threads are very popular in machine artwork, and the quality of these threads has improved dramatically from what it was a few years ago. We are also seeing unusual threads used, such as needle punch yarn, fine baby knitting yarns, and perle cottons. Once you have learned the basic stitching techniques and have total control of your sewing machine, I would suggest that you purchase a variety of these threads and use them to experiment with the different techniques. You can become as creative as you want, and have the skill to achieve any look you desire.

When threading the machine with nylon thread, care must be taken that no drag is put on it. If you have constant tension and/or breakage problems when using nylon thread, use a cone holder or a small jar that will hold the cone upright on the table, off the machine, and allow the thread to come off from the top of the cone. Place the thread on the right side and in back of the machine. If no thread guide is available at the spool pin area of the machine, tape a closed safety pin onto the machine at the spool pins. Also tape a closed safety pin along the back of the machine so that the thread will track as if it were coming off the spool pins themselves.

Tip *When these specialty threads are used, you may find that regular needles do not produce the quality of stitch you desire. Be sure to study the section on machine needles in Chapter One to help you select the correct needle for the thread you are using. A wonderful reference on decorative threads is Maurine Noble's book* Machine Quilting with Decorative Threads.

Jean Stitch™, Wooly Nylon™, and Cotty™ (size 12) are just a few of the heavier threads that have found their way into the machine arts world. These threads need to be threaded through a topstitching needle, size 90 or 100. They give a nice look to Blanket stitch appliqué.

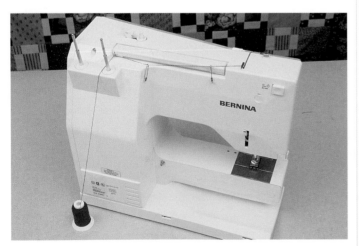

Threading system for nylon thread, using safety pins

Decorative threads that may be used

Thread Usage Suggestions

80/2 Embroidery thread
- Size 60 or 65 needle
- Bobbin thread
- Heirloom sewing
- Machine embroidery

60/2 or 50/2 Embroidery thread
- Size 65, 70, or 75 needle
- Bobbin thread for all machine appliqué techniques
- Satin stitch appliqué (in needle)
- Straight edge appliqué (in needle)
- Machine embroidery
- Buttonholes in garments
- Machine quilting when quilting very close ($1/2$" or closer) with cotton in the top as well as in the bobbin

30/2 Embroidery thread
- Size 70, 75, or 80 needle
- Blanket stitch appliqué (in needle)
- Open decorative stitches
- Heavy fill in embroidery

.004 nylon
- Size 60 needle
- Invisible Machine appliqué (in needle only)

Scissors

A great deal of cutting is necessary in appliqué, and high-quality scissors will make it much easier. I suggest that you experiment with different types and sizes of scissors for this work.

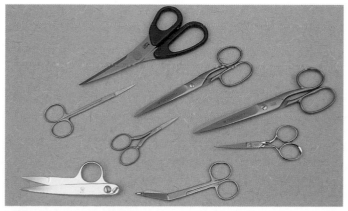

Different styles of scissors

You need to have a really sharp and high quality pair of paper scissors. When cutting paper, sharp scissors are necessary so that the edges of your paper templates and patterns are smooth and even, not chewed and curled, as often happens with dull or inappropriate scissors. Your paper-cutting scissors and skills are just as important as the cutting of the fabric, even more so in appliqué.

Tip *Did you know that cutting paper with your good sewing scissors does not hurt them? Since paper is made of cellulose and so is fabric, cutting freezer paper, pattern paper, and bond papers does not damage knife-edge scissors. This does not mean you can cut cardboard and plastic with them!*

For cutting larger pieces and cutting the seam allowance around freezer paper, many quilters still prefer to work with Ginghers®, but I personally like to work with Clover® Patchwork and Dovo® scissors. The Clover Patchwork scissors have a very fine serrated blade that holds a single thickness seam allowance like a third hand. These scissors allow you to trim one thread at a time if necessary, without the blades slipping. They are lightweight and comfortable. The crème-de-la-crème of scissors are the German-made Dovo brand. These are excellent cutting tools and they come in a variety of shapes and sizes.

When clipping curves and points, a very sharp point on small scissors is critical. Make sure that the pair of scissors you choose feels good in your hand, and cuts right up to the very tip of the point.

Many people find that a pair of 4" curved-blade embroidery scissors are helpful for cutting circles and curved areas.

A small pair of appliqué trim scissors (bandage scissors) is very helpful when cutting away the back of invisible Machine and Straight-edge appliqué. They have a rounded, wedge-shaped bottom blade that glides along the stitching, measure a $1/4$" seam allowance, and there are no points to accidentally cut through the front of the appliqué.

Above all—sharp scissors are a must!

FYI: Gingher® appliqué scissors are used when trimming around a stitched item where cutting very close to the stitching is necessary. They are mainly used for reverse appliqué techniques and are not meant to be general-purpose scissors. The storkbill-shaped blade lies flat on the fabric to create resistance for the cutting blade when cutting close to the stitching. These scissors are not needed for any of the techniques in this book.

Tip *When cutting, practice moving the paper or fabric, not the scissors. This will leave smoother edges. Also, try taking large bites with the blades to give a longer, more continuous cut. Small scissors make small chops and can leave uneven edges.*

Fabrics

Appliqués consist of fabric pieces applied onto a fabric background. For Satin-stitch technique, beginners will find sturdy, woven, 100% cotton fabrics the easiest background fabric to use. In general, the appliqué fabrics should be lighter than, or equal to, the weight of the background fabric of the project.

Grainline is not particularly important on smaller appliqués, but when working with large pieces, match the grainline of the appliqué to the grainline of the background fabric. This is especially important if you are going to wear or hang the finished product, or if it is not going to be quilted within the appliqué itself.

Test your fabrics for colorfastness before starting to work with them. Depending on the fabrics' colorfastness to water and detergent, you can pre-wash them or not.

Note: For detailed information concerning colorfast tests and options, refer to Chapter Eight in *From Fiber to Fabric.*

If the item you are appliquéing is going to be laundered, decide whether to pre-shrink it. If you are appliquéing onto a pre-shrunk garment, you will need to pre-shrink the appliqué fabrics. If the item is going to be quilted, you may choose not to pre-shrink to obtain an antique look.

If you do choose to pre-wash, do not apply spray starch or fabric sizing to the fabric when working with freezer paper techniques, as these products diminish the adhesive properties of the freezer paper. Some people prefer to work with softer, pre-washed fabrics; others prefer the sizing and body of a new fabric. Try working with both, and see which method gives you superior results.

Often the combination of fabrics and fusibles used in appliqué can shrink in varying degrees, causing unsightly puckers and wrinkles. If necessary, make a sample using the chosen fabrics and fusibles; then wash the sample to see how they react.

Medium weight 100% cotton fabrics are the easiest to work with when doing Invisible Machine appliqué techniques. They are very easily turned and manipulated, and they hold a crease well. Polyester blends and other synthetics tend to be more wiry and make it harder to turn an edge and keep it there; however, the freezer paper techniques presented here will make it easier to work with these more difficult fabrics.

Fabrics of 100% cotton are easiest to work with when applying heat-fusing products. Be careful of heat-sensitive fabrics when using fusibles. They may not be able to withstand the hot temperature required for the fusing process.

Fusibles

Fusibles are agents that adhere one fabric to another. They come in various forms, each requiring a different method if application. I recommend that you purchase small amounts of several and "test" them to determine appropriateness to your fabrics and projects.

Tip *To store, sort the fusibles into envelopes or reclosable bags, labeling with product name and instructions. Add the tests to your sample book with notes on the product, fabric, and application method.*

Fusible Webs

(Stitch Witchery®, Fine Fuse™, Tuf-Fus™)

Stitch Witchery and Fine Fuse are durable fusible webs that come by the yard. Stitch Witchery gives a firm, almost stiff feel to the finished item, while Fine Fuse leaves the item soft and pliable. Both Stitch Witchery and Fine Fuse launder very well; there is sufficient adhesive agent to hold the fabrics together if directions are followed carefully. Use only low-heat settings when tumble-drying items.

Fusible webs melt between two layers of fabric, creating a permanent bond. Care must be taken when working with these products, as they tend to stray and easily melt onto irons and ironing board covers. They used to be tedious to work with because they had to be cut to the exact size as the appliqué itself, but the Teflon® pressing sheets have made them much more acceptable and easy to handle, with very good results.

When fusibles were introduced, along with them came non-stick pressing sheets. These sheets of heat-resistant material create iron-on fabric and make it possible to work with these fusibles without getting the fusible on the iron and ironing board. They come in several sizes and two different grades. The professional grade is more durable and long lasting; the larger the sheet, the more useful it is.

Once paper-backed fusibles became available, many people stopped using these products because they were harder to work with and messier. However, the bonding agents on the paper backing products are often uneven in thickness, making your appliqué release in places. The webs maintain a uniform thickness and are manufactured to be lightweight, resulting in a soft appliqué that does not release.

Paper-Backed Fusible Webs

(TransWeb™, Wonder-Under™, HeatnBond®, Appliqease™, Steam-A-Seam®)

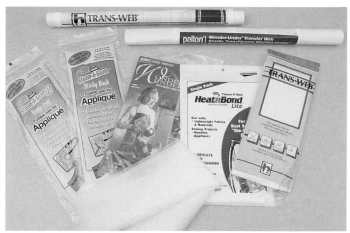

Paper-backed fusibles

These products came along after the fusible webs. They are a polyamide web on release paper. HTC Trans-Web and Pellon Wonder-Under are similar to fusible webs, but with the addition of a paper backing that makes pattern tracing and cutting much easier. They are easy to use. Basically, the pattern units are traced onto the paper side. Using a preheated iron on a medium setting, the fusible is place on the wrong side of the fabric and pressed on the paper side for about 1–4 seconds. (An overheated iron may cause an insufficient bond). Once the piece is cut out, peel the paper away, place the fusible side of the motif on the right side of the background fabric and press for 3–5 seconds to bond.

HeatnBond is a 100% solid sheet of glue for a very strong bond. This product is ideal for bonding delicate fabrics and lightweight materials where a lower temperature is necessary with a shorter pressing time. It is more washable and dry cleanable than the webs.

Appliqease and Steam-A-Seam are sticky on both sides, thus making them repositionable. Once the glue side is adhered to the fabric and the piece cut out, the second piece of paper is removed, exposing a tacky surface that can be repositioned before ironing permanently in place.

Fabric Spray Temporary Adhesives
(505® Spray & Fix, KK2000™, Quilt Basting Spray)

Fabric Spray Temporary Adhesives

The commercial embroidery industry introduced spray adhesives to the quilt market. Fabrics can be repositionable if spray is allowed to dry a bit first, but can be permanent if used immediately after spraying. I find these products a bit messy, but they are popular and worth your time to try them. Be sure to read the label before use.

♥ **HINT: Test-sew all of the above products to see if they gum up your needle. If so, use rubbing alcohol to clean the needle.**

Non-Stick Pressing Sheets

Non-stick pressing sheets

These sheets made of heat-resistant material can be ironed onto directly, so that applying fusible webs to fabrics is much simpler than before. We no longer have to cut the pieces separately, then realign them and hope they don't move as the iron comes down. Now the design is drawn directly onto the fusing agent, then placed onto a piece of fabric, and covered by the pressing sheet. The iron is on the pressing sheet, fusing the web onto a piece of fabric. The fusing agent cannot stick to the sheet, so it can be easily peeled upon cooling. Then the appliqué is cut out on the line.

Pressing sheets are generally translucent and are used in various steps for preparing fabric. You can buy them in a variety of sizes, as well as by the yard (a large size is handy for larger projects). A professional-grade pressing sheet will last for years. Any fusing residue left on the pressing sheet should be brushed off to prevent it from getting on the iron or fabric where it does not belong. Keep your pressing sheet clean.

Teflon pressing sheets are excellent for protecting napped fabrics and metallic and rayon threads when pressing. Place the pressing sheet on top of the fabric instead of pressing directly on the fabric's surface.

Glues

Fabric Basting Glue Sticks

Various glue basting products

Fresh glue sticks are effective when working with the small seam allowances required of some techniques. Be sure to work with fabric-basting glue sticks instead of paper glue sticks. Textile glue comes in a stick form similar to a lipstick and can be found in fabric and quilt stores. It is made from nontoxic and water-soluble glue, often with a touch of Teflon, which makes it glide onto the fabric easily. If your glue stick becomes gummy or stringy, replace it with a new one. GLUE STICKS SHOULD BE 100% WATER-SOLUBLE AND ACID-FREE.

The glue sticks that I have found easiest to work with have a translucent glue. If the glue is white, it is apt to be gooey and sticky, making it very difficult and messy to work with. The glue should glide onto the fabric easily and smoothly, with no lumps. Be sure to look for acid-free glue stick so that there is less chance of a chemical reaction between the glue stick and the fabric dye. When this happens, color transference problems can occur onto the background block.

Glue sticks are useful for holding anything that you might otherwise have to pin or baste—especially points, corners, and curved edges. Tiny pieces that cannot be pinned are easier to handle with glue sticks.

Tip *Store glue sticks in the refrigerator or freezer in a sealed recloseable bag. Work with one when it is cold. If it becomes gummy or warm, put it back in the freezer and take out a cold one. The heat of your hand or the humidity in the air can make it very messy to work with. Keep a wet washcloth beside you to keep your fingers clean.*

Roxanne's Glue Baste It® is great to use for temporarily holding appliqués in place on the background fabric instead of using pins. It is 100% water-soluble, but is thick enough to allow a tiny dot to bead and hold the piece firmly until it is stitched. It comes with a very small needle-like applicator that allows you to really control the amount that is released.

Stabilizers

There are basically two different types of stabilizers—temporary and permanent. Temporary stabilizers are removed after the stitching is finished. These stabilizers need to be strong enough to support the fabric and stitches, and still have the ability to tear easily in both horizontal and vertical directions, without putting stress on either the background fabric or the stitches. Temporary stabilizers are the most favored for appliqué and will be discussed in detail in this section.

There are several non-woven nylon or polyester products sold as background stabilizers. These products are not fusible and may or may not become a permanent part of the appliqué. They are used underneath the background fabric to give extra body and support for Satin stitching to prevent tunneling and puckering. Permanent stabilizers are either cut away after stitching, or they always stay in the project.

Temporary stabilizers come in a variety of styles and formulations, with different glues, fibers, and chemicals. They are used to add support to lightweight fabrics, especially when doing Satin stitch appliqué.

There are three basic types of temporary stabilizers: tear-aways, water soluble, and heat sensitive.

Temporary Stabilizers
(NoWhiskers, Easy Stitch, Stitch-N-Tear®, Stiffy™, Tear Easy™, Totally Stable™, Tear-Away™, Press & Tear™, freezer paper)

Temporary Stabilizers

TEAR-AWAYS

Tear-aways are removed by gently pulling them away from the stitching. The stabilizer should tear away cleanly in both directions, leaving no fibers sticking out from the stitches. If the product you are using has a high percentage of polyester or rayon, leftover fibers are more likely to occur. The cellulose variety are like paper; the fibers are laid in a web, which allows them to tear easily.

> *Tip* *These products come in light, medium and heavy weights. A general rule of thumb is, the lighter the fabric, the heavier the stabilizer needs to be. However, it is sometimes preferable to use two or three layers of a light weight tear-away for extra support rather than to use the extra thick variety. The thicker types tend to leave more of the fiber residue within the stitches after they are torn away.*

Press and Tear and Sulky's Totally Stable are iron-on tear-away products with a plastic coating on one side. They keep knits and unstable fabrics from stretching while stitching and also eliminate shifting, sliding, and puckering of fabrics, and leave no residue when the excess is torn away. You can iron a soft, flexible stabilizer onto larger projects as well as onto sweatshirt fleece and knits. It sticks like freezer paper until you tear it away, and it keeps its flexibility while working.

Freezer paper is another good stabilizer. Plastic-coated freezer paper hit the quilting world several years ago and revolutionized the way we prepare appliqué pieces. You will find this paper at your grocery store or at your local quilt shop. The paper is fairly durable, easy to fold and cut, transparent for tracing, and gives perfect edges to appliqué pieces.

The plastic side can be ironed onto the back of the background fabric and then torn off after stitching. The plastic does not damage the fabric in any way and peels off easily, with no residue, when you are finished. Once ironed on, it helps eliminate shifting and fabric stretching. It is stiff and best suited to smaller Satin-stitched projects.

I have often used junk mail and paper as a stabilizer when Satin stitching. Adding machine tape, freezer paper, parchment paper and clean newsprint are some of your options.

WATER-SOLUBLE STABILIZERS

(Aqua-Solv, Solvy™, Magic, Sol-u-web™, RinsAway™)

Rinse-away products

These products have been used in machine arts for several years and have found their way into quilting. These products (except RinsAway) are water-soluble embroidery facings made of a gelatinous substance. They are easy to use and dissolve by spraying or soaking in cool water. They are especially helpful for placement marking of detail lines for Satin stitch. They can be used on top or underneath and are especially useful on napped or pile fabrics, such as corduroy, towels, knits, and velvets. By stitching over the stabilizer, the stitches are less likely to become buried in the nap of the fabric. When the project is finished, gently tear away any excess, and spray lightly with water or steam to dissolve the remaining film. Be certain to carefully read the instructions before using, as some of these products have specific needs for removal. Two or three layers can be pressed together to create a firmer backing. Use a press cloth or Teflon pressing sheet to do this. Store these products in an air-tight plastic bag to prevent humidity from ruining them.

RinsAway can be used on the back as a stabilizer on washable projects when you don't want to tear it off. You can let it dissolve when the item is laundered. It also substitutes for freezer paper as a template material.

HEAT SENSITIVE BRUSH OFF STABILIZERS
(Heat-Away™, Clear N Melt, Heat 'n Brush)

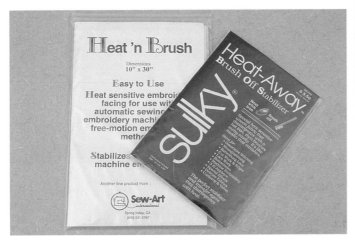

Stabilizers removable with heat

These stabilizers are the answer when wetting or tearing would cause distortion to stitches or damage fragile fabrics. They are well suited for wearable art and machine embroidery. Resembling stiffened gauze, heat sensitive products can be used on the top or on the bottom of the project. Once the stitching is completed, the stabilizer will disintegrate by placing a dry, hot iron (cotton or linen setting) on it until it turns brown–about 10–15 seconds. Gently brush away the brown residue with a soft brush. Be sure to follow the instructions carefully.

Liquid Stabilizers
(Fabric Stabilizer, Magic Sizing®, Starch)

These products are used to paint onto the edge of shapes or for dipping fabrics into. They stiffen the fabric and keep the edges from fraying when sewing.

Templar, Tag Board and Template Plastic

Tag board and templar

Templar® is a heat-resistant template material available at quilt stores. It is used for the Invisible Machine and Straight stitch appliqué techniques where the seam allowance can be pressed over the template instead of glued over the edge of freezer paper. Because it is specially treated, it will not melt like plastic.

Tag board is another excellent medium for making templates because it is easily cut, readily available, and can also be used with an iron. It is sold in large sheets in art supply stores. You can also use heavyweight manila file folders.

Template plastic is used to make templates when many units of the same size need to be traced. You might find it easier to make a set of templates and draw around them over and over than to trace each unit over and over. This will also help retain the integrity of the shape each time it's drawn.

Marking Tools
You need a supply of pencils with smooth leads (a number $2^1/_2$ works fine with no smearing). A good quality mechanical pencil is easy to work with and always has a sharp point. Be sure that the pencil is comfortable in your hand, enabling you to trace accurately and easily. Pencils will be used for freezer paper applications. When working with fusible web papers, pencils tend to smear so fabric marking pens and fine-or medium-point permanent black markers are preferable. Avoid using ballpoint pens.

Transparency Film

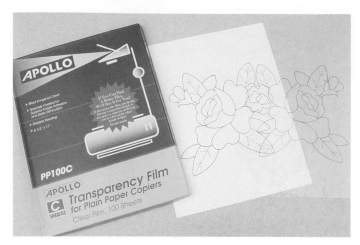

Transparency film

Transparency film is a specially coated, clear acrylic sheet that can be run through photocopy machines, ink jet printers, and laser printers to assist in the pattern tracing process. Be sure to buy the type that is appropriate to the machine you are using. Using this film eliminates the need to retrace designs in mirror image. Simply copy the design onto the film, and you can just turn it over to get an automatic mirror image of the design. Great for tracing, and also useful for layout.

Pins

Different types of pins

Look for pins that are very fine in diameter so that the appliqué pieces lie as flat and smooth as possible when pinned in place. Iris™ Swiss Super Fine Pins (1¹/₄" long) or Clover Appliqué Pins® (¹/₂" with glass heads) are excellent for this.

CHAPTER 3

Machine Basics

Basic Machine Maintenance

A well-maintained machine will give you many hours of pleasure. Before starting any sewing project, be sure to clean and oil your machine. The best brush is the one that came with your machine, and the best cleaning solvent is rubbing alcohol. Because it evaporates quickly, it doesn't promote rust. Dip your brush into it and remove the lint, old oil, and other debris in the machine.

Cleaning the Machine

- Thoroughly clean the bobbin area and the feed dog area with the lint brush or small paintbrush, dipped in rubbing alcohol.

Tip *A 1/2" wide paint brush with the bristles cut down to about 3/4" in length makes an excellent cleaning brush.*

Often the smallest amount of lint or debris will cause the machine to skip stitches and have tension problems.

- Use brushes and pipe cleaners to remove lint from every reachable area.
- Tweezers can be used to remove caught threads, but otherwise avoid using metal tools to clean with, as they can create burrs that can cause thread breakage.
- Remove the needle plate and clean the lint from between the feed dogs.
- Scrub the feed dogs with a toothbrush.
- Use a vacuum to suck away loose particles, then use the blower or a hair dryer to blow out the tiny particles not removed by suction. Remember to always blow away from the inside of the machine rather than into it.
- Clean between the tension disks with a pipe cleaner or a piece of soft cloth. Dip either one into rubbing alcohol and run it gently between the separating disks of the upper tension mechanism. Do this about every six months to remove any excess sizing, coating, dye, or other buildup that thread might have shed there. Make sure the presser bar lifter is up. Remember to do both sides if you have double disks (for two threads).

❋ The pressure spring on the bobbin case may contain lint or pieces of thread that can cause tensions to vary and cause poor stitches. Run a piece of heavy thread dipped in alcohol under the spring.

❋ Clean the inside of the bobbin case, as lint buildup can cause the bobbin to spin unevenly, and affect the quality of the stitches.

❋ Clean the body of the machine by wiping the surface with a soft cloth dampened with rubbing alcohol. Wax it with a high-quality car wax for enameled steel parts and a kitchen or plastic product wax for any plastic parts. Be sure to keep the machine covered when not in use to prevent accumulation of dust and dirt particles.

Oiling the Machine

❋ Lightly oil the shuttle and race of the bobbin area every time you clean it. Use only high-quality, pure sewing machine oil, purchased from your sewing machine dealer.

▼ Note: Good sewing machine oil has no detergents. Regular machine oils will eventually cause the mechanisms to become gummy or lock up. Do not spray silicone or products such as WD-40 into the machine because they over-spray, and many parts need to be completely free of lubricant.

❋ Once a month, if you are sewing a great deal or doing a lot of appliqué work, put a drop of oil on the needle bar (take the needle out before oiling). Let the machine run for two minutes after applying the oil, then let it sit for 10 minutes so the excess oil can drain off. When not sewing, lower the needle into soft cotton fabric so that any excess oil can wick into the fabric.

As far as your machine is concerned, the best relationship you can have is with your mechanic. Good communication about how you plan to use your machine and what products you plan to use goes a long way toward keeping your machine performing at its best. Long periods of fast sewing, such as Satin stitch requires, can make it necessary to lubricate the machine more often than you normally would. Listen carefully to the sound of your machine when it is well oiled. When you begin to hear the sound change–generally a rough and noisy sound–it is telling you it needs more lubrication. Ask your mechanic to go through your machine with you and show you every place where you need to add oil. Even though many machines are sold as non-oiling, there is no such thing. The bobbin area generally needs oil added regularly, so make sure you know where and how to do it correctly.

Replace the Needle

After you have oiled the machine, put in the proper needle. Refer to Chapter Two about needles to make sure you select the proper type and size for your project. Check in your manual to see if the flat side of the needle goes to the back or to the side.

❋ To insert the needle, push it up until it hits the stop, and then tighten the screw until firm. Do not apply too much pressure on the needle clamp screw. You could easily break off the point that holds the needle in place. If the needle is not inserted properly, the machine will skip stitches, if it will sew at all.

❋ When sewing, listen to the sound of your machine. Any time that you hear a punching sound, stop and change the needle.

❋ It is important to check for burrs occasionally. A burr is a tiny, rough area on the needle, generally caused by pulling the fabric through the machine from the back, or by hitting pins. Either of these can cause the needle to strike the throat plate, often breaking the needle. A burr can interfere with the glide of the thread as it travels through the machine. It can affect the quality of the stitches, cause snags in the fabric, and even cut the thread.

❋ Check the condition of the throat plate. It is fairly common to see chipped areas which create a rough edge along the inside of the opening. This can cause problems with broken threads, as they come in contact with the edge and the thread is cut. Replace the throat plate if it has too many burrs to smooth away.

※ Burrs are best removed with a piece of crocus cloth (very fine sandpaper made of jeweler's rouge impregnated in fabric). These fibers are so fine they will smooth out burrs without creating new rough spots. You can find this cloth at hardware stores.

※ Run your fingers over all the metal parts of your machine. When you find a rough spot, remove it. Don't overlook the shuttle area. It is harder to find and remove burrs from this area, but it can be one of the most bothersome areas for thread breakage.

Tension

Many sewers find themselves going into a cold sweat when you just mention tension, let alone talk about adjusting it. In reality, there isn't anything mysterious about setting and adjusting the thread tensions on your machine. It's mostly a matter of not having been shown how to do it. What can be very confusing are the many problems that appear to be tension-related, but are really caused by factors other than mis-adjusted tension settings. Keep this checklist handy for troubleshooting before you start to change your tension settings.

First if all, is the machine threaded correctly? Incorrect threading is responsible for more "tension" problems than any other single item. Make sure you check your threading for the following:

※ All the thread guides are used

※ You threaded with the presser foot up

※ The thread is unwinding smoothly from the spool (it will often get caught on the slash on the side of the spool)

※ You are not using a bobbin as a source for the top thread

※ The bobbin is threaded and inserted correctly

※ The bobbin is filled correctly

※ Remove any thread on the bobbin before you wind on new thread.

※ Follow instructions carefully for winding a bobbin. It needs to be evenly and tightly wound with the proper tension.

※ Do not let any thread wrap around the edge of the bobbin, or any tail extend beyond the side of the bobbin.

※ Wind at a consistent and slow speed. This is more important with polyester and nylon threads than cotton because of their stretch.

Non-threading checklist:

※ Is the machine clean? Lint and thread ends lodged between tension discs, under the throat plate, or in and around the bobbin case can all increase the resistance and restrict the thread flow.

※ Check for damaged machine parts.

※ Check for bent needles or bobbins.

※ Check for rough areas on thread guides, needle eyes, tension discs, throat plates, bobbin case and the shuttle hook.

The smallest damage can distort tension. Cut thread close to the tension spring on the bobbin case before removing bobbin. Raising the presser foot before removing thread from the upper tension helps prevent damage. Needles, thread, and fabrics must be compatible; using different thread sizes and types in the bobbin and top can throw off basic tension settings.

Also a needle that is too large or too small for the thread can unbalance the stitches. The size of the hole adds to or reduces the total top tension.

Adjusting the Top Tension

In order to understand tension, you need to have a working knowledge of the tension tools on your machine.

※ Identify the tension adjustment dial on your machine. When doing any type of machine artwork, you need to become comfortable with tension adjustments to make the machine work properly with different types and combinations of threads.

※ When you want to form a row of stitches that looks the same on both sides of the fabric, the same amount of thread needs to flow from the spool and the bobbin simultaneously. This is achieved by running the threads through various tension devices on the machine head for the upper thread, and the bobbin case spring for the bobbin thread.

❋ The tension discs and tension regulator together are called the tension assembly. The discs squeeze the thread as it passes between them, while the tension regulator controls the amount of pressure on the discs. Older machines have two discs controlled by a screw or knob, newer machines have three discs (also called double disks) controlled by a dial or sensor system within the computer. The presence of three discs allows you to sew with two threads at once if you like.

❋ The tension regulator is easy to understand. When adjusted to a higher number, the discs move closer together, thus increasing the amount of pressure on the thread. If the dial is turned to a lower number, the discs spread apart, decreasing the pressure.

❋ The thread guides on the machine each exert a small amount of resistance on the thread, adding to the tension from the discs. Always make sure that all guides are threaded before stitching. Review your machine's manual if you are unsure of the proper threading system.

❋ When using thick threads without a tension adjustment, the pressure will increase and cause the upper thread flow to decrease. Some newer machines make automatic upper-tension adjustments. Because the bobbin case is not self-adjusting, the lower tension may need to be adjusted manually to match the top.

Bobbin Tension Adjustments

The flat spring on the side of the bobbin case exerts pressure on the thread as it comes out of the bobbin case. A small screw regulates the amount of pressure at the end of the spring. This can be easily located if the bobbin case comes out of the machine. If the machine has a built-in bobbin case (you drop the bobbin into the machine), it can be a bit more challenging to locate the screw. This is where a trip to your mechanic for instructions and guidance is really helpful.

The screw is turned clockwise to tighten or counter-clockwise to loosen. Turn the screw in small increments and never more than a quarter turn between tests.

If you are uncomfortable with making adjustments to your bobbin case, you might want to invest in a spare case. Mark it with nail polish and keep it for specialty stitching. That keeps your other bobbin case ready for normal stitching.

Now let's put this into practice.

Checking the Tension on Your Machine

When the tensions are balanced, the stitched line looks good (the same) on both sides of the fabric (a). If you see visible knots or loops on either side of the fabric, you will know that the tension needs adjusting. If the needle thread shows on the back side, the needle tension is too loose or the bobbin is too tight (b). When bobbin thread shows on the top side, the needle tension is too tight or the bobbin thread is too loose (c).

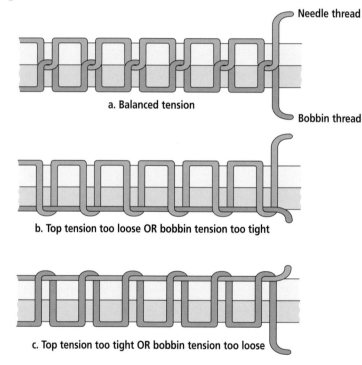

a. Balanced tension

b. Top tension too loose OR bobbin tension too tight

c. Top tension too tight OR bobbin tension too loose

Effects of tension adjustments

Whenever you switch from your regular sewing thread to another type of thread, first thread the machine and test your setup to see what adjustments need to be made. If you can get away with only adjusting the top tension—great! If that doesn't work, however, the bobbin case will also need to be adjusted.

For the appliqué techniques in this book, you will be using very thin threads compared to normal sewing threads. This will undoubtedly create the need for some minor tension adjustments.

- Place a full bobbin into the bobbin case. Make sure it is threaded properly (check your manual).

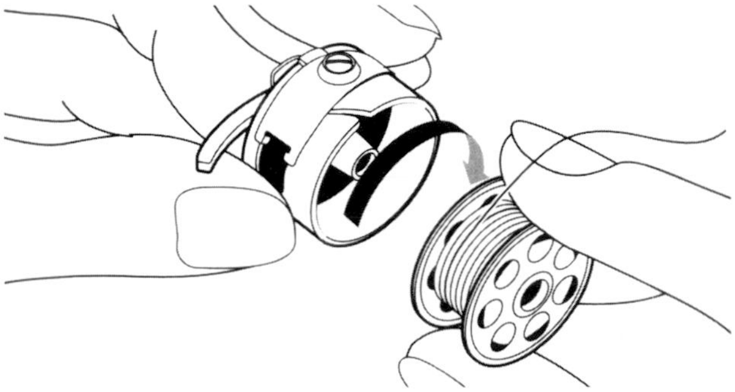

Insert with thread running clockwise

- To begin, let the bobbin case hang freely by the thread. It must not slide down by its own weight, but when you jerk your hand lightly upward, yo-yo style, it should gently fall. If it doesn't move at all, the tension is tight. If it falls easily, it is loose.

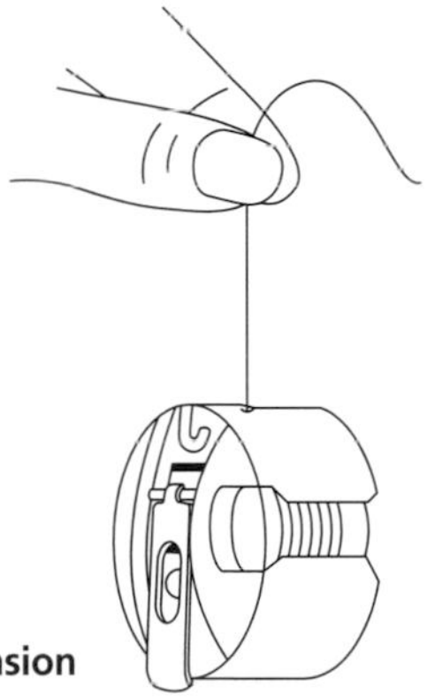

Test for normal tension

- Thread the top of the machine with your chosen thread.
- Insert the correct needle for the thread size and weight, as well as the usage.
- Sew a length of stitches, using the technique you plan to be working with.
- Compare the result with the illustration on page 30.
- If you see any bobbin thread showing on the top, loosen the top tension one number. Try again.
- Continue loosening the top as necessary, until you see loops of top thread start to form on the underneath side of the fabric. This is an indication that the top is too loose, and now needs to be tightened up until those loops go away.
- If you still see bobbin loops on top, it is a clear indication that the bobbin case needs to be adjusted more tightly.
- Adjust the bobbin tension by adjusting the large screw on the tension clip.
- Turn it to the right to tighten, and to the left to loosen. Remember the saying—"righty tighty, lefty loosey."
- Adjust in small increments until the tension is correct. Read the screw like a clock, and move only one hour at a time, never more than a quarter of a turn at a time.

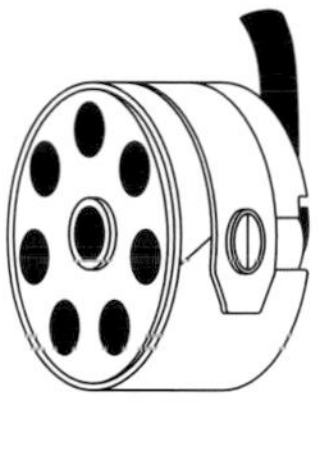

Tension screw on bobbin case

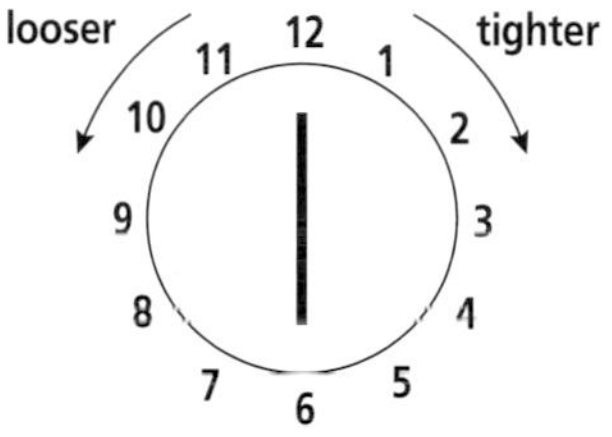

Make adjustments in small increments—think of hours on a clock

Tip *I always keep a pad of self-stick notes beside my machine to make notes to myself. No matter how hard I try, I forget what changes I made to the bobbin screw almost the minute I made them! (Senior moments really play into tension adjustments). Begin by making a drawing of the clock face shown above on the note pad. Holding your bobbin as in the above illustration, draw a line to represent the position of the screw before any adjustments are made. Then write a note to yourself as to how you read that line–as if it were time. In the illustration, it could be either 12:00 or 6:00. Once you have made the necessary adjustment, draw another line in a different color ink to show the new position. Now write a note to yourself that states: I moved the screw to the right from 12:00 to 4:00. This will make perfect sense a few days later when you are ready to take the tensions back to normal. If you don't make the note this elementary, you won't have a clue what you did, or how to get it back!!*

When doing machine artwork such as appliqué, using very thin size 50 or 60 2-ply threads, the bobbin tension will generally need to be tightened to get the proper drag on the thread.

When trying to achieve a perfect Satin stitch, the top thread should be pulled down to the underside. This requires a tighter-than-normal bobbin and a looser setting on top.

 If you are using a Bernina or Viking 1+, insert the thread into the hole in the finger of the bobbin case. This will automatically tighten the bobbin tension.

MACHINE TROUBLE-SHOOTING

Beyond the basic root causes of machine problems above, I have added the information below as a reference. There are so many little things that can make us crazy using our machines, and most of them can be corrected easily.

Problem: Sewing machine suddenly stops during sewing
Cause: Machine has been run at a low speed for an extended period of time
Solution: Turn power off and wait about 20 minutes. Safety device will reset, and machine will be ready to operate

Problem: Needle will not move
Cause: Bobbin winder shaft is in winding position

Problem: Upper thread breaks
Cause: Threading is not correct
          Thread tension is too tight
          Thread take-up lever is not threaded
          Needle is inserted wrong
          Needle is wrong size
          Needle type and thread do not correspond
          Needle is bent or blunt
          Hole in the throat plate is chipped or has sharp edges
          Starting to stitch too fast

Problem: Bobbin thread breaks
Cause: Bobbin has not been fully inserted into bobbin case
          Bobbin has been incorrectly threaded
          Bobbin tension is too tight
          Bobbin is wound too full
          Bobbin does not turn smoothly in bobbin case
          Lint in bobbin case or shuttle
          Throat plate hole is damaged

Problem: Skipped stitches
Cause: Thread tension too tight
          Thread take-up lever has not been threaded
          Needle is wrong size
          Needle type and thread do not match
          Needle is bent or blunt
          Pressure too light on presser foot
          Timing could be off from sewing over pins or breaking a needle

Problem: Irregular/unattractive stitches
Cause: Improper threading
          Loose upper thread tension
          Incorrect needle size
          Needle type incorrect for fabric being sewn
          Needle incorrectly inserted
          Pressure too light on presser foot
          Unevenly wound bobbin
          Pulling fabric while stitching

Problem: Fabric puckers
Cause: Stitch length is too long for material
          Needle point is blunt
          Incorrect thread tension
          Pressure too light on presser foot
          Fabric is too soft—needs stabilizer
          Using two different sizes or kinds of thread

Problem: Jamming of thread
Cause: Upper and lower threads are not drawn back under presser foot
Feed dogs are lowered

Problem: Needle breaks
Cause: Needle has not been fully inserted into needle bar
Needle clamp screw is loose
Using straight stitch throat plate in zigzag mode
Pulling fabric as you sew
Incorrect presser foot
Bobbin is overfilled
Tension too tight on upper thread

Problem: Knocking noise
Cause: Dust has accumulated in feed dogs
Lint is in hook
Thread caught in shuttle

Problem: The machine does not feed material
Cause: The stitch length has been set to zero
The presser foot pressure is too low
Feed dogs are lowered
Threads are knotted under fabric

Storage

When you are not using your machine, do not cover it with plastic. If any humidity is present, the machine could sweat under the plastic, causing possible rust formation. Simply cover the machine with a towel or quilted cover to keep the dust away. If the machine has been unused or in storage for a period of time, be sure to take it in to a mechanic to be totally cleaned, oiled and adjusted before expecting it to operate at its top potential.

The more you understand how your machine operates, and what it takes to keep it in top working condition, the more hours of trouble-free enjoyment you will get out of it.

CHAPTER 4

Preparing the Pattern for Satin and Blanket Stitching

Before you start choosing fabrics and cutting pieces out, you will need to take time to analyze the pattern you are working with.

Working with Patterns

Satin stitch and Blanket stitch appliqué techniques both use raw-edge preparation methods. That edge is prepared with a fusing agent to keep the fabric edges from raveling and to give a stable edge to stitch over. The pattern pieces need to have seam allowances added where there are overlapping units.

♥ **Note: Blanket stitch can be done over a turned edge, and if that is your choice, refer to Chapters Eleven and Twenty for instructions on pattern preparation and turning edges over templates.**

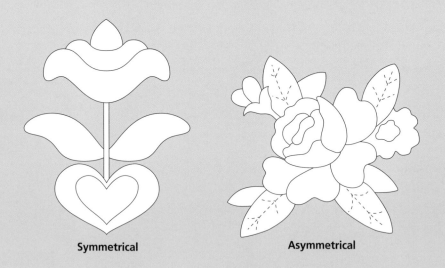

Symmetrical   **Asymmetrical**

Symmetrical or Asymmetrical?

First, look at the pattern for the Love Tulip on page 58, or the pattern you are planning to work with. Is the design (a) symmetrical (identical on either side of the center), or (b) asymmetrical (directional – each side is different)?

Methods for Tracing Patterns

You will need to understand the principles of mirror image or reverse image to work with asymmetrical patterns. If the pattern is not traced properly, the picture or design will be facing the opposite direction of the original pattern when the fusing process is finished. If you are working with a symmetrical pattern, you simply trace the pattern onto the fusing agent's paper side as the pattern is drawn. If the pattern is asymmetrical, however, you will need to trace the reverse of the original. This can be done a couple of different ways.

One method is to re-trace the pattern onto the backside of the paper it is printed on. Be sure to mark back and front on each unit. You would next trace the backside (reverse) tracing onto the paper side of the fusing agent.

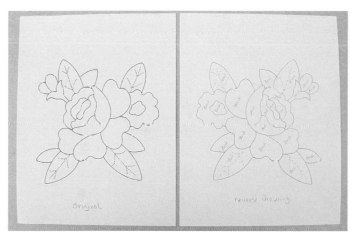

Pattern retraced on back

USING A PHOTOCOPY MACHINE

Another way that eliminates the re-tracing process is to utilize a photocopy machine. The first time I saw this idea used was in the instructions from the Curiosity line of patterns. This method uses transparency film, which is readily available from office supply stores. Be sure to buy the correct type for the type of copier you are using. This clear film can be run through the copier and the toner prints onto the surface, making the pattern reversible by simply turning the acetate sheet over. This is a very accurate way to work with complex designs where many pieces are involved. If the design does not fit on one sheet, break the pattern into units and copy each unit on a separate sheet. The sheets can be taped together if needed for tracing.

Using transparency film

Analyzing the Pattern Unit Combinations

After you understand mirror imaging, next analyze the pattern to determine if any of the units can remain large shapes, with the detail lines stitched in, instead of cutting separate pieces of fabric for every detail. This is easily done when Satin stitching the unit onto the background fabric, as the Satin stitch becomes the design line instead of a fabric edge. An example is the rose pattern on page 36. Some of the flower's fabrics can be cut as larger units using the outside lines, and the petal segments can then be drawn and then stitched in.

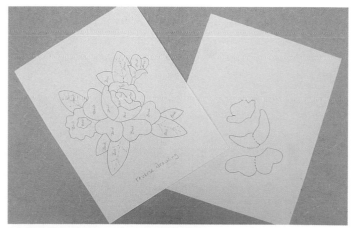

Combining pattern units to make one piece

Adding Extensions for Underlapping

Wherever two pattern pieces come together, one of the pieces must be under the other. The under-lapping edge needs to have an extension of ⅛"– ³⁄₁₆" added. We never want to "butt" two raw edges together. The under-lapping piece is the one that appears to be behind as you look at the pattern. Often, you will need to consider if lighter-colored fabrics should lie under darker ones.

Draw these extensions onto the pattern in red before tracing the pattern. This will remind you to add them to each pattern piece, where they are needed, while tracing onto the fusibles.

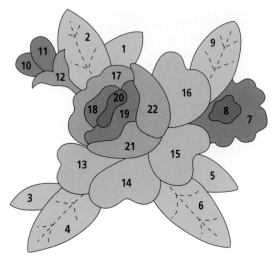

Each piece numbered separately

Extensions drawn

Numbering the Pattern Units

You might also want to consider numbering all the pattern units. When there are multiple layers, I start by numbering the bottom-most pieces. These would be the first pieces to be positioned onto the background fabric. As you work upward to the top-most layer, the numbers get larger. This will help you keep track of each unit's relationship to the others. It will also assist in determining which pieces will be stitched first, and their progression. Study the pattern at the right to see the numbering system.

Some pieces numbered as larger units.

You can see that once the pieces are numbered, it is easy to check and see if you missed any pieces that need an extension added.

Now the pattern is ready to trace onto your preferred paper-backed fusing agent.

CHAPTER 5

Working with Fusibles for Satin and Blanket Stitching

Once you have your pattern prepared as discussed in Chapter Four, you will need to decide which fusing agent and technique you prefer. This chapter will walk you through the methods required by each different type of product, then give you various techniques of preparation for the pattern pieces.

How to Use Fusible Webs

1. Start by drawing the desired pattern shapes onto the fusible, using a felt-tip pen or blue wash-out marker. Draw carefully so that you do not tear the web.

2. Cut apart the different units leaving about ¹/₂" beyond the drawn lines. Do not cut the designs on their lines at this point.

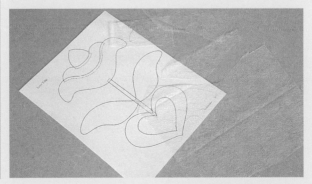

3. Place a Teflon pressing sheet on the ironing surface.

4. Next lay the appliqué fabric right side down on one half of the pressing sheet, then lay the fusible web on top of the fabric. Have the reverse image facing you if applicable.

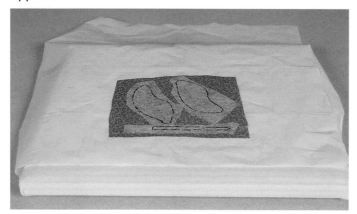

5. Cover both the fabric and fusible web with the remaining half of the pressing sheet.

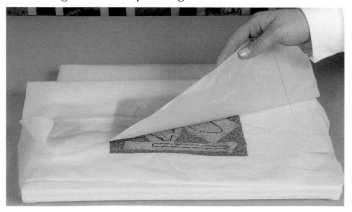

6. With your iron set on the wool setting, press the layers for 5-10 seconds. (Do not slide iron.) The adhesive cannot adhere to the pressing sheet, so it can only adhere to the fabric.

7. Allow the pressing sheet to cool, then peel it away from the fused fabric. You now have a fusible fabric.

8. Cut out the design on the line, handling the item very carefully to avoid stretching the edges, which causes fraying. You now have an "iron-on" appliqué.

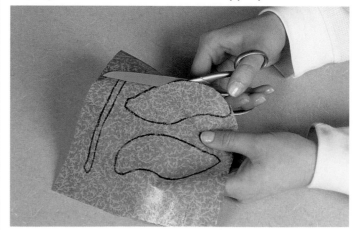

9. Position the appliqué onto the background it is to be stitched to (refer to Chapter Six for information on rebuilding the design). With your iron on the steam and wool setting, press for 10 seconds.

If you are using a dry iron, use a damp pressing cloth. The non-stick pressing sheet is not necessary for this step, but the use of a damp pressing cloth will strengthen the bonding process. Read the instructions that come with the particular product you purchase to double-check on its requirements for heat and moisture. Now choose a stabilizer and the appliqué is ready to be stitched.

How To Use Paper-Backed Fusible Webs

Before you begin, carefully read all instructions that come with each product. Follow suggested pressing temperatures and times for each product.

1. Start by tracing the design shape directly onto the paper side of the fusible. Remember to draw in reverse image if working with an asymmetrical design.

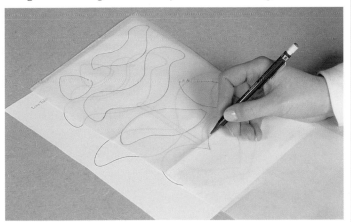

 To protect the ironing surface from any stray fusible, position the non-stick pressing sheet under the fabric.

2. Lay your appliqué fabric right side down on the ironing surface. Place the rough side of the fusible against the wrong side of the appliqué fabric. Press for three seconds with a hot dry iron. Do not slide the iron. Let the fabric cool.

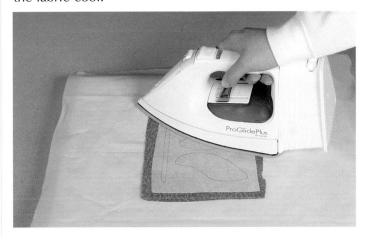

3. Cut out the shape on the line, making very smooth, even cuts. Handle the pieces carefully.

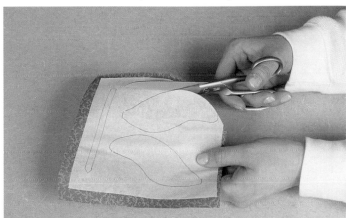

4. Gently peel off the paper backing, taking care not to stretch the edges of the appliqué. Place the appliqué, adhesive side down, onto the right side of the background fabric and press with a hot iron. After choosing a stabilizer, the appliqué is ready to stitch.

How to Use Double-Stick Fusible Webs

Double-stick fusibles such as Steam-a-Seam 2 and Appliqease provide the flexability for you to reposition the cut fabric pieces before permanently fusing them to the background fabric. Just remember, the more you handle your pieces, the greater the risk of frayed or stretched edges.

These products have a pressure-sensitive coating on both sides of the web. This allows it to temporarily stick to the appliqué material, then adhere the appliqué piece to the background. The entire appliqué can stay in place without shifting, and is repositionable until pressed with an iron. Once you are completely satisfied with the design, your fabric choices, and the layout, all of the appliqué pieces are fused in one step by ironing them to the background.

It is recommended that fabrics be pre-washed to remove sizing and other chemicals that may prevent the fabric from bonding to the web. If you prefer to not pre-wash your fabrics—for whatever reason—I recommend that you work with the regular paper-backed fusibles discussed on page 21.

The steps to using double-stick fusible webs products are similar to the paper-backed webs.

Check to see which paper liner removes first by peeling a small section apart at a corner. Do not remove. Trace (in reverse if necessary) on the opposite side, then remove the other liner. Stick the web to the appliqué fabric. Cut on the line. Peel off the remaining paper liner—the one you traced on—leaving the web on the fabric, and stick the appliqué onto the background fabric. You can now reposition as needed or desired. Once everything is positioned correctly, press for 10-15 seconds.

▼ **Note: One complaint about these two products is that the sewing machine needle tends to get gummed up when stitching through them. If you are using these products and that occurs, keep a cotton ball and rubbing alcohol close to your machine and frequently wipe the needle with it to remove the residue.**

Eliminating Stiffness When Working With Fusibles

For years quilters have fought against using fusible webs because of the added stiffness of the finished pieces. This isn't such a problem on simple designs, crafts, pillows, etc., but on quilts, clothing, and multi-layered appliqués, the less pliable feel is objectionable. It becomes too stiff to quilt, while losing the soft hand and drapability of lovely handmade quilts.

When I wrote the first edition of *Mastering Machine Appliqué*, I addressed this problem in the Blanket stitch chapter. I was reluctant about doing Blanket stitching at all if I had to put up with stiffness in my quilts. Jeanne Hutchinson of Northfield, Vermont, acquainted me with a method of using fusible seam tape that overcame this problem. She fused small pieces of the tape over the pattern line, then cut the piece out. What she had was the center, free of any fusing agent, but edges that were fusible. I tried this, but lost patience working with pieces of hem tape and the pressing cloth. Static electricity was my biggest enemy. In desperation, I came up with the idea of using paper-backed fusible web, but adapting it to her method. This has since become a standard method of working with paper-backed fusibles in quiltmaking.

1. Again, prepare the pattern pieces as discussed earlier. Trace the appliqué design onto the paper side of the fusible. Remember to check whether you need to trace in reverse or not.

2. Cut the fusible $1/8"$ to $3/16"$ inside the line you have drawn. You will be cutting the center of the appliqué design away. Do not cut on the line.

3. Leave a margin of fusible on the outside of the line. This will be cut away in the next steps. Fuse the pieces onto the wrong side of the appliqué fabric.

4. Carefully cut along the drawn line, keeping the edges smooth.

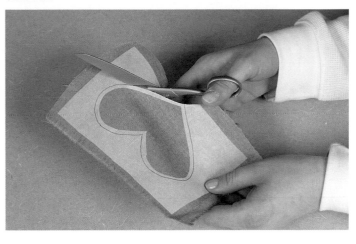

5. Gently and carefully tear the paper off the fusible that is left along the edge.

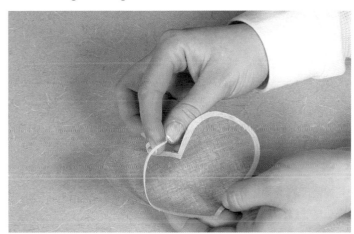

CHAPTER 6

Building the Design

By now you have chosen your pattern, fabrics, and fusing method. Once you have all your fusible pattern pieces affixed onto the appliqué fabrics, you are ready to reassemble the units into the design.

Using Fusibles

There are many different thoughts about how to prepare an appliqué for stitching. Many people draw the design onto the background fabric, then position the pieces over these lines. I personally find this method risky. First, if there is any size discrepancy between the pieces and the drawn design, the line will show beyond the pieces. It is possible this line will not come off. You will also have problems when you have multi-layered designs. Once the bottom pieces are in place, you can no longer see the lines for positioning other pieces.

If you try to place the pieces by eye, you risk distorting the finished design. It is very difficult to place multiple pieces by guessing. I have found that rebuilding the design using the pattern as a guide, with or without the background fabric, gives me the most accurate finished piece. We will use the Tulip pattern on page 58 for this exercise.

Begin by placing the complete pattern on a hard ironing surface. If the pattern you are working from is just half or a quarter of the design, you will need to copy the pattern (twice if working with half the design, or four times if working with a quarter). Tape them together so you have an accurate complete design.

1. If you can see the pattern clearly through the background fabric, place the pattern under the background fabric and fuse the pieces directly onto the background.

2. If you can't see through the background fabric clearly, cover the pattern with a large Teflon pressing sheet. You will be able to see the design lines through the pressing sheet. You will build the pattern on the pressing sheeet, peel it off when built, then apply to background fabric.

3. Start by identifying the bottom layer. Carefully remove the paper from the fusing agent on the back of each piece, and position it exactly on top of the placement lines of the pattern. Position all the bottom layer pieces that do not touch. Very carefully press with a heated iron for just a few seconds. This will fuse these pieces either onto the background fabric or the pressing sheet. By doing this, they won't be as likely to slip out of position as more pieces are positioned.

4. Identify the next layer of pieces that will go on top of the extensions of the bottom layer pieces. Before placing them on the pattern, remove the paper from the fusing agent on the back of each piece. Carefully position the pieces—one at a time—on top of the lower pieces. When they are in their exact position, carefully place a heated iron on the section that is overlapping. This will attach this layer of pieces to the bottom layer pieces. Continue with each additional layer, peeling the paper off and fusing in place.

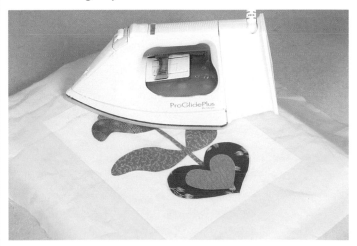

5. If you needed to work with the pressing sheet, let the entire design cool before carefully lifting it off the pressing sheet. It should now be one complete unit. Position the design onto the background fabric, and press again with a heated iron. Now the entire design is fused onto the background.

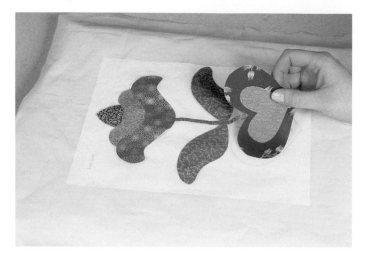

Tip *Working with multiple layers is difficult when the pattern is underneath the appliqué pieces. The appliqué pieces hide the design lines. Instead, photocopy the pattern onto a sheet of transparency film (acetate). Tape the top of the acetate onto the background fabric and place the appliqué pieces between the two. You will be able to see when the appliqué piece is not in the correct position, as the pattern is on top of everything.*

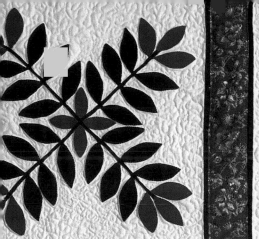

CHAPTER 7

Machine Preparation for Satin Stitching

Now that you have read the first three chapters, you should have a good understanding of the equipment and supplies needed to achieve beautiful appliqué. If you are still unsure about needles, thread, tension adjustments, or anything else about your machine, please go back and review those topics until you are more comfortable with the concepts.

We will begin by sewing several samples so that you can become very comfortable with the machine adjustments and stitching techniques before you begin a project.

Supplies needed:

- 60/2 cotton embroidery thread for bobbin (white, gray, or black)
- 60/2 or 50/2 cotton embroidery thread for top—contrasting color to appliqué fabric
- 70/10 Universal point needle
- Open-toe appliqué foot
- Fabric—for appliqué and background
- Fusing agent of your choice
- Stabilizer

Practicing

You need to be very familiar with the stitch width and length regulator location on your machine. Since you will be adjusting the stitch width as you work, your hands should know where to go automatically without taking your eyes off the appliqué. Also be familiar with the sensitivity of the knob or button.

Setting the Machine up for Satin Stitch

The needle position for the majority of Satin stitch appliqué is the center position. Put the open-toe appliqué foot on the machine; thread the bobbin case with a bobbin containing 60/2 thread. Thread the top of the machine with 50/2 or 60/2 machine embroidery thread in a contrasting color to the fabric on which you are going to stitch your test sample. Insert a size 70/10 Universal needle in the machine.

A Satin stitch consists of narrow zigzag stitches set close enough to appear as a solid line, but not so close that they bunch up and jam in front of the foot. The Satin stitch completely encloses the raw edge, preventing raveling. It has a crisp, durable-edge finish that, in turn, gives a well-defined image. This is totally different from the softer edge obtained with Invisible Machine appliqué techniques which use a turned-under edge.

SETTING THE STITCH LENGTH

Using two layers of fabric and a background stabilizer such as freezer paper, stitch a few rows and adjust the width to about ⅛" wide. Adjust the length to the shortest stitch you can, without allowing the fabric or thread to jam up. The machine should feed the fabrics evenly without help (don't pull on the fabric or you will distort the stitches).

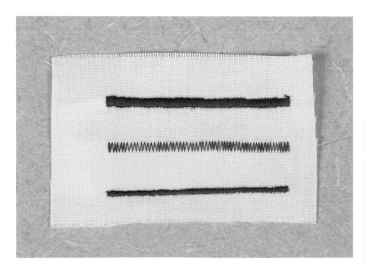

Satin stitches of various lengths and widths

Tip Gaps tell you that your stitch length is not set close enough. If the fabric jams up, the stitches are set too close together. I strongly suggest that you sit on your right hand for awhile, and just guide with your left. Let the feed dogs do all the feeding. It will seem like the fabric is barely moving—because it is! We have a tendency to overdrive and/or push the fabric as it passes under the foot, causing the formation of uneven stitches. This makes it difficult to tell if the machine is having trouble, or if you are just helping it too much. Guide with your left hand only, and have your right hand at the ready to adjust stitch width when needed.

SETTING THE STITCH WIDTH

The ridge of Satin stitches should be wide enough to completely encase the raw edges of an appliqué piece. This will prevent raveling through multiple launderings. Each swing of the needle should catch approximately five to seven threads of the appliqué fabric. This is generally ⅛" wide or smaller. Start by setting your machine on a width of 2. Try not to let the stitches get too wide, or the appliqué will have a bulky, heavy look. ⅛" is sufficient to hold the edge securely without raveling. If the stitches are too wide—curves, corners, and points are more difficult.

SETTING THE TOP TENSION

When you have found width and length settings you are happy with, the top and bottom tensions need to be adjusted. Most appliqué techniques use different weights of threads in the needle and bobbin case. You will start to compensate for this situation by loosening the top tension slightly. The buttonhole tension setting on the top tension dial is a good place to start. This action will draw the top thread to the underside, giving a smoother appearance along the edges.

SETTING THE BOBBIN TENSION

Sew a line of stitches and look at them. There should be no bobbin thread showing on the top side. If there is, you probably need to tighten the bobbin tension as well as loosen the top. If the top tension gets too loose, the stitch will loop. You want a tight stitch, where top thread color shows on the bottom but no bobbin thread shows on the top. This way, you do not have to constantly change the bobbin thread to a color that matches the top thread. It is more economical and a real timesaver!

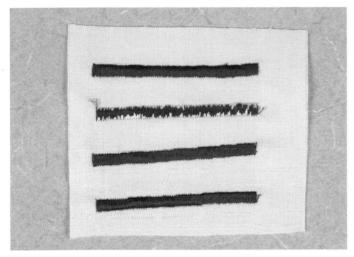

Stitches made with different tension settings

Next look on the backside of the fabric. If the tension has been adjusted adequately, there should be a bar of bobbin thread running down the center of the stitching on the wrong side of the fabric, or, there might be color on one side only.

Don't forget that you may need to readjust the tension for different sewing conditions. The weight and thickness of the fabric, number of layers, thread size and quality, spool size, and even how the thread is wound on the spool all affect the thread tension. Regularly check the back of your work to be sure that the threads remain properly balanced. (Refer to page 30 for detailed information on tension.)

Next, test different stabilizers. Even with the tensions set correctly, the heaviness of the Satin stitching can pull the fabric inward between the needle swings, causing a tunneling effect in the fabric.

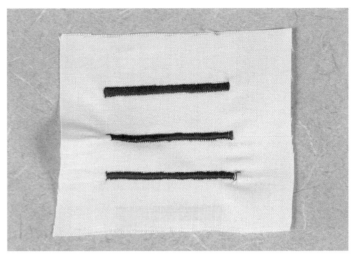

Tunneling

Tunneling can result in distortion of the background fabric and a puckered appliqué. Using a sturdy enough stabilizer eliminates this. Generally, a heavy fabric needs a lightweight stabilizer, but a lighter-weight fabric needs a sturdier, stiffer stabilizer. Practice Satin stitching with different combinations until you feel comfortable with the products discussed on page 23 and the combinations needed to obtain flat, even stitches and appliqués. You will find that stitching without stabilizers not only creates tunneling, but the machine will not feed the fabric evenly, will often stretch the fabric as it feeds, and you will have uneven stitches.

Making Adjustments as You Sew

Now you need to learn to control the fabric with your left hand, while making width adjustments with your right hand.

Guiding fabric with left hand

While sewing a line of Satin stitches, turn the width dial very slowly to a narrower then a wider width, going to the extreme each way. Then turn the dial quickly. The more slowly you make the adjustments, the more elongated the tapers will be. If the dial is adjusted quickly, the tapers are choppy. You will encounter points and angles requiring both types of adjustments, so get comfortable with changing the width as you sew.

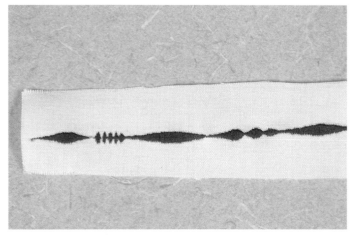

Stitch width adjusted while stitching

Now move the needle position to the right. Again, sew a line of stitches and adjust the width dial. The stitches will appear flat on the right side and will get wider to the left side. If the needle position is moved to the left, the left side of the stitches will be flat and will widen to the right. This is useful in achieving the look of mitered corners and for any number of decorative uses.

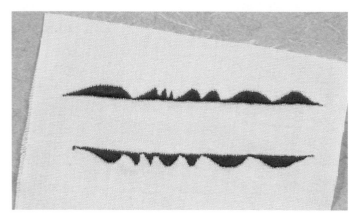

Needle position affects stitch width changes

Tip *Check the stitch tension as you taper. Often the bobbin thread will appear on the top when you go into a very narrow stitch. Tighten the bobbin and loosen the top in very small increments until you have corrected this problem.*

Once you have practiced enough to be comfortable with the tension adjustments and width and length settings, you can progress to the next chapter and learn the stitching techniques.

CHAPTER 8

Satin Stitch Appliqué Techniques

Now that your machine is set for Satin stitching, the next step is to prepare the shapes on pages 135-136 using a fusible and fabric. Refer to Chapter Five for preparation techniques, and then practice the stitching techniques explained here.

Stitching Techniques

These exercises will help you obtain perfect points (both inside and outside), corners, curves, and miters. Practice these techniques on scraps of fabric, then move on to a design of your own choosing. Soon you will be doing perfect Satin stitching! Remember to add the samples you are about to make to your sample notebook, with the appropriate notes.

When you have the shapes cut out and fused onto a background fabric, place a piece of freezer paper, or other stabilizer of your choice, behind the background fabric.

Locking Off the Thread at the Beginning

Pull the bobbin thread up

Whenever possible, begin stitching in the center of a straight line or gentle curve. Try not to begin stitching at a point, corner, or curve. Pull the bobbin thread up to the top of the fabric by taking one stitch, making sure that the machine's thread take-up lever is at its highest position.

Needle positioned correctly on edge of appliqué

Pull on the thread, and the bobbin thread should come up through the needle hole. This allows you to hold both threads to eliminate any possible thread jams as you start stitching. Holding both threads in one hand, take several very small, straight stitches. This locks the thread in place. Cut the thread tails close to the surface of the fabric.

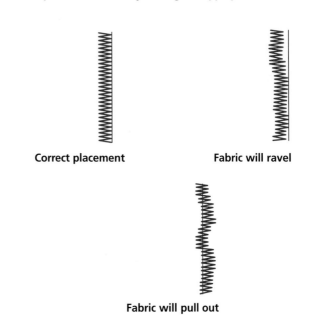

Correct placement   **Fabric will ravel**

Fabric will pull out

Hold both threads to avoid jamming

When Satin stitching, the ENTIRE STITCH WIDTH IS ON THE APPLIQUÉ. When the needle is in the right-hand swing or position, it should be just rubbing the edge of the appliqué. Train your eye to watch the needle as it swings to the right with each stitch, and keep the needle and appliqué edge aligned at all times. If the needle is too close to the edge, a frayed, hairy edge results. If the needle is too far from the edge, the edge will not be secured adequately and the Satin stitch will not appear smooth.

Practice Using Various Shapes

Straight Lines—Using Shape #1

Practice positioning the needle on the edge of the appliqué by stitching down both sides of the bar shape you prepared. Do not worry about turning the corners on this example.

Corners—Using Shapes #2 and #3

Outside corners are the easiest elements of appliqué to maneuver. When you get to the corner, allow the right-hand swing of the needle to fall just off the appliqué edge into the background fabric, and just off the front edge of the appliqué. Do not stitch even one stitch beyond the raw edges.

OUTSIDE "CROSSOVER" CORNER

1. Stitch until the appliqué piece is completely covered and the needle is just off the edge of the appliqué corner.

Step one

2. Stop with the needle in the fabric in the right-hand swing, and pivot 90°. The next stitch will be made manually so it will fall on the Satin stitch instead of on the background fabric.

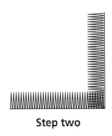

Step two

Using the hand wheel, take a stitch so that the needle is in the left position, and position the fabric so that the needle is just barely in from the edge of the Satin stitching. The first stitch will be barely on the Satin stitching. Continue stitching on top of the Satin stitching, crossing over it.

OUTSIDE "BUTTED" CORNER

This technique is used when you need the corners of two opposite sides to match.

1. Stitch until the appliqué piece is completely covered and the needle is just off the edge of the fabric. Stop with the needle in the left swing and pivot 90°.

2. Take the next stitch manually, turning the hand wheel until the needle is in the right swing. The needle is now aimed into the background fabric, not along the edge of the appliqué.

3. Reposition the fabric so that the needle will go into the hole the top thread is coming out of. This allows the new line of Satin stitching to "butt" up against the previously stitched edge, without crossing over. Instead of a stacked appearance, it gives the effect of stitching both sides of an end first, then the end itself.

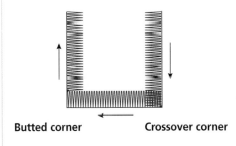

Butted corner   **Crossover corner**

OUTSIDE MITERED CORNER

If your machine has both right-and left-hand needle positions, you can do mitered corners.

1. Set your machine in right needle position. Stitch down the edge to the corner. At the corner—stop.

2. Lower the needle into the background fabric at the exact corner of the appliqué piece where the stitching stopped. The needle should be in the right-hand swing.

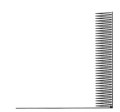

First side of outside mitered corner

3. Pivot. Turn stitch width to 0. Position your right hand on the stitch width lever. Stitch slowly, while gradually increasing the stitch width. Because of the right-hand needle position, the width will only increase to the left, making a 45° angle as you stitch.

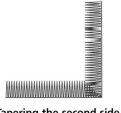

Tapering the second side

When you get to the edge of the left side of the first row of Satin stitching, you should be back to your original stitch width. This technique will take a bit of practice.

Practice this technique on the last two corners of the shape. Lock your stitches at the end.

MITERED OUTSIDE CORNER USING BUILT-IN STITCHES

If you have a triangular decorative Satin stitch on your machine, you can use it to create really nice corners.

Triangular decorative stitch

1. Stitch to the corner with a normal bar of Satin stitching. At the corner, pivot and then engage the triangular stitch. If you have a pattern-stop function, also engage it. This should make the machine start the stitch at the point, widening as it stitches. (Some machines also have a function that stops in the center of a decorative stitch. If you have this function, engage it also).

1/2 of stitch

2. When you get to the widest point of the triangle, stop stitching.

Mitered corner using triangular decorative stitch

3. Re-program your machine back to the original Satin stitch and continue on the straight edge.

INSIDE CORNERS

1. Stitch to the raw edge at the bottom of the corner. Continue to stitch past this point until you have gone into the body of the appliqué as far as the stitch is wide.

Step one

2. Stop the needle in the left-hand position. Pivot 90°. The first stitch in the new direction should be made taking one stitch manually, moving the hand wheel of your machine. This positions the needle in the right swing position. The needle should be aligned with the upcoming edge when it swings to the right.

Move the fabric just a fraction so that the first stitch will be just barely inside and on top of the sewn stitches. This prevents the first stitch from making a loop behind the first bar of Satin stitching. The needle should also be aligned with the new raw edge to be stitched. Cross over the corner, and continue stitching down the raw edge.

Step two

Scalloped Inside Corner— Using Shape #4

SCALLOPS WITH BUTTED CORNERS

Step one

1. Stitch past the cut point as far as the width of your Satin stitch. Pivot with the needle on the left side.

Step two

2. Raise the presser foot and with the right-hand swing of the needle lined up with the upcoming raw edge; continue stitching. Be careful that the stitch does not fall behind the previous line of stitching.

SCALLOPS WITH MITERED CORNERS

These inside corners can also be mitered.

Step one

1. Draw a faint line from the point of the corner (outside edge) to a mark that is as far in from the edge as your stitch is wide. Try using your left-hand needle position for this technique. Keep your hand on the stitch width dial or button as you stitch the first side of the corner. Slowly decrease the width to 0 as you come to the mark.

Step two

2. With the needle in the fabric, pivot, and slowly increase the width as you stitch out toward the edge of the appliqué. When the right needle swing is back to the cut edge, you should be back to the original width setting.

Curves—Using Shapes #5 and #6

Pivoting is necessary when stitching around curved areas. It allows you to realign the edge of the appliqué with the needle as the fabric changes direction. Without pivoting, slanted stitches appear, giving the edge a messy finish. REMEMBER THAT THE STITCHES SHOULD ALWAYS BE PERPENDICULAR TO THE CUT EDGE OF THE APPLIQUÉ.

Problems resulting from improper pivoting:

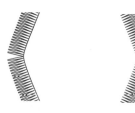

a) Gaps from pivoting on the wrong side of the needle swing

b) Slanted stitches from not pivoting

To change the direction of your stitching by pivoting, simply stop the machine with the needle in the fabric and raise the presser foot, then reposition the fabric so that the stitches will once again be perpendicular to the cut edge of the appliqué. Only a very slight turn of the fabric is necessary. You will know when to pivot when you find that you cannot align the fabric fast enough while stitching to prevent slanted stitches. You will feel like you want to push the fabric.

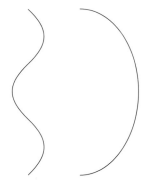

Stitching gentle curves

A large or gentle curve will require only two or three pivots; often with practice, running the machine at full speed, these slight curves can be done beautifully without pivoting at all. More frequent pivoting is necessary on tight curves.

OUTSIDE CURVES

As you are stitching along the curve of the design, you will see the line of stitching start to move away from the curve. This is when you need to pivot. Pivot with the needle in its right-hand swing, into the background fabric.

On an outside curve, the needle is on the outside of the appliqué piece. Lift the presser foot slightly, and move to reposition the fabric slightly so the stitches barely overlap as you continue to stitch the edge.

Positioning points for outside curves

You might find it helpful to stitch a few stitches (counting them), then pivot again. Continue this until the ring is completed, and lock off the stitches.

INSIDE CURVE

Inside curves are treated similarly to outside curves, except for the needle pivot position. You pivot inside curves when the needle is on the left-hand side of the stitch, or on the appliqué fabric. Inside curves are often tighter than outside curves, so you will need to do more pivoting. Go slowly and count the stitches. It is almost like a chant—4 stitches and pivot, 4 stitches and pivot (or however many stitches you can take before needing to pivot).

Pivoting points for inside curves

Remember: Pivoting while the needle is on the wrong side of its swing leaves gaps in the row of stitching. Pivoting when the needle is on the correct side of its swing allows the thread to stack up slightly, creating a solid line of even stitches. No pivoting at all leaves slanted stitches that are unattractive and don't secure the raw edges properly.

Points—Using Shapes #7 and #8

Points can be tricky and perfect inside points almost elusive. But, with lots of practice these elements become fun and they showcase your stitching skills. Start with the inside points.

BLUNT INSIDE POINTS

When learning to stitch inside points, it is helpful to draw a line from the upcoming edge on the other side of the corner into the body of the appliqué for a guide. Eventually, you will be able to do this by eye, without the line.

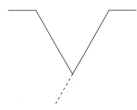

Line drawn for inside point

1. Stitch the edge to the bottom of the "V" where the fabric is cut. Continue stitching into the fabric until the left swing of your needle hits the line you have drawn as deep as the width of the stitch used.

You will be stitching straight until your needle hits the line you have drawn.

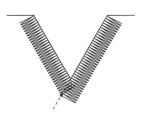

Step one

2. Pivot, and reposition the fabric. To do this, allow the needle to swing to the right and leave it in the up position. Move the fabric so that the needle will go down into the same hole the thread is coming out of. The foot and needle should now align with the raw edge of the other side. Continue stitching.

Step two

If the first row of stitching is not deep enough into the fabric, the stitches will not overlap and will give you two blunt ends of stitching. The cut point is not secured and the fabric is likely to fray and ravel after a few washings.

Incomplete inside point

If you stitch too deeply into the fabric when you pivot, the stitching will cross over into an "X", leaving two ends out of alignment. Practice will correct both of these problems.

Cross over inside point

POINTED INSIDE POINTS

With a wash-out marker, draw the shape the Satin stitch needs to make on the inside point. Once you have guidelines drawn, you can taper the stitches to give a pointed effect.

1. Stitch until the needle hits the line marked on the right side. Pivot the fabric slightly so that the foot and point are aligned. Gradually reduce the width of the stitch to match the lines drawn. At the end of the point, you should be at "0" width.

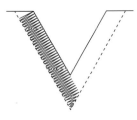

Step one

2. Pivot. As you stitch up the next side of the point, gradually widen the stitch to normal, and pivot slightly to accommodate the angle of the edge.

Step two

You might also want to work with the left- or right-hand needle positions again to help make more accurate points.

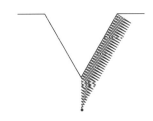

Using right and left needle positions

TAPERED OUTSIDE POINTS

These points are easy to understand, but they take a bit more practice to perfect.

1. Stitch along the raw edge, keeping the width consistent until the needle is just beginning to stitch beyond the raw edge of the left side of the point. Pivot the fabric slightly to bring the point into the center of the foot. This will help prevent a curve from forming.

Step one

2. Gradually decrease the width of the stitch as you sew. Your guide here is to always have each needle swing rub both raw edges. The taper of the point dictates the amount by which you decrease. The stitch width should never be wider or narrower than the point. By the time you are at the very end, you should be at "0" width and the point should be totally encased with stitches. Pivot.

Step two

3. Stitch out of the point by increasing the stitch width at the same rate that you decreased it. The width will increase as the width of the point increases. When you have returned to normal width and the needle is no longer on the left edge, pivot slightly with the needle. Continue stitching. This technique works especially well on long, thin points.

Step three

MITERED OUTSIDE POINTS

1. For a mitered look, you will need to gradually reduce the stitch width as you approach the point. You should only stitch to the halfway mark of the fabric in the point, instead of stitching over it completely, as in the technique above.

Step one

2. Once you have reached the end of the point, lower the needle, pivot, and continue to stitch the other side by gradually increasing the stitch width until you are back to the original width.

Step two

Again, you might want to experiment with the right needle position to see if you can become successful in narrowing the stitch on only one side.

Locking Off Threads at the End of Stitching

Once you have returned to where you started, or at the end of a piece, you must lock off the thread tails. If you are coming back around to where you started the stitching, as with the "L" shape, stitch two to three stitches on top of the first ones. Then change your needle position to the right, and set the stitch width to "0". Stitch several tiny, short stitches "in the ditch" of the Satin stitch. They cannot be seen there and are very secure.

If you are stopping at the edge of another fabric, stitch three to four stitches into the next fabric and stop. Cut the threads. When you stitch the next fabric, the Satin stitching will cover these end stitches and lock them in.

"Invisible" Zigzag Stitches

Debra Wagner is known for this type of appliqué on her award winning quilts. She does not care for Invisible Machine appliqué with the Blind stitch, but true Satin stitching is too heavy and bulky for her style of quilts. She uses The Invisible zigzag stitch on both turned-edge and raw-edge appliqué.

Invisible zigzag stitches are formed much like Satin stitches. They are merely a simple zigzag. The difference is that here there is a gap between the stitches instead of being a solid bar of stitching. Set your machine width at 1.5 and the length at 1.0 to try this technique. Practice points, corners, and curves; then start to reduce the stitch width and length. The size of the zigzag is dependent upon your skill. The smaller the stitches, the less conspicuous they are. Debra recommends that the smallest stitch settings for a turned edge be .75 width and .5 length. For raw-edge appliqué she suggests no smaller than 1.0 width and .75 length.

Corners and curves are handled exactly the same as Satin stitch. Try all the methods and choose your favorite.

Checking for Errors

After you have stitched your samples, look at them closely and compare your work to the illustrations shown throughout this chapter. Check to see if you have any of the problems indicated. Take the time to practice and correct any mistakes you find before moving on to an exercise.

When mistakes are made on a project, correcting them by taking out the stitches is easier than you would imagine. Use a seam ripper and work from the wrong side. Cut through the bobbin thread only, and from the top, pull on the top thread. The stitches should unravel easily.

Exercise

When you are comfortable with the stitching techniques, apply your new skills to the Love Tulip pattern on page 58. Use the information in Chapters Four and Five to prepare the pattern pieces for stitching.

Place the pattern units for the tulip on the background fabric and a piece of your chosen background stabilizer on the back. Press in place if needed; otherwise pin in place.

1. Begin by stitching the leaves. They are beneath the stem, so they are the units farthest to the back. You can take the first couple of stitches on top of the stem, as they will be locked off when the stem is stitched.

2. The ends of the leaves have acute curves, so take special care to pivot enough to keep the Satin stitching smooth. Stop the stitching a couple of stitches into the top of the stem again. You can do this any time you will be stitching over the ends with another line of stitching, such as the ends of the stem, the bud, and the small petal.

3. The stem is stitched next, since its ends are under the flower and heart.

4. Now stitch the smaller heart onto the large heart. Review the techniques for stitching inside and outside points.

5. Stitch the two hearts onto the background fabric. Remember to lock off the stitches when completing each of the hearts, because there will be no other stitches going over them to capture the tails.

6. The bud at the top of the flower is next.

7. Continue with the small petal, then the large petal. Remember to lock off the stitches when completing the large petal, because there will be no other stitches over them to capture the tails.

You have now created a beautiful Satin-stitched appliqué. The more you practice these techniques, the more skilled you will become. Satin stitch is a lovely way to embellish many items, and is strong enough to be used on garments, as well as baby quilts and other items that need frequent washing. Almost any appliqué pattern can be adapted to Satin stitch, so explore and have fun!

Love Tulip

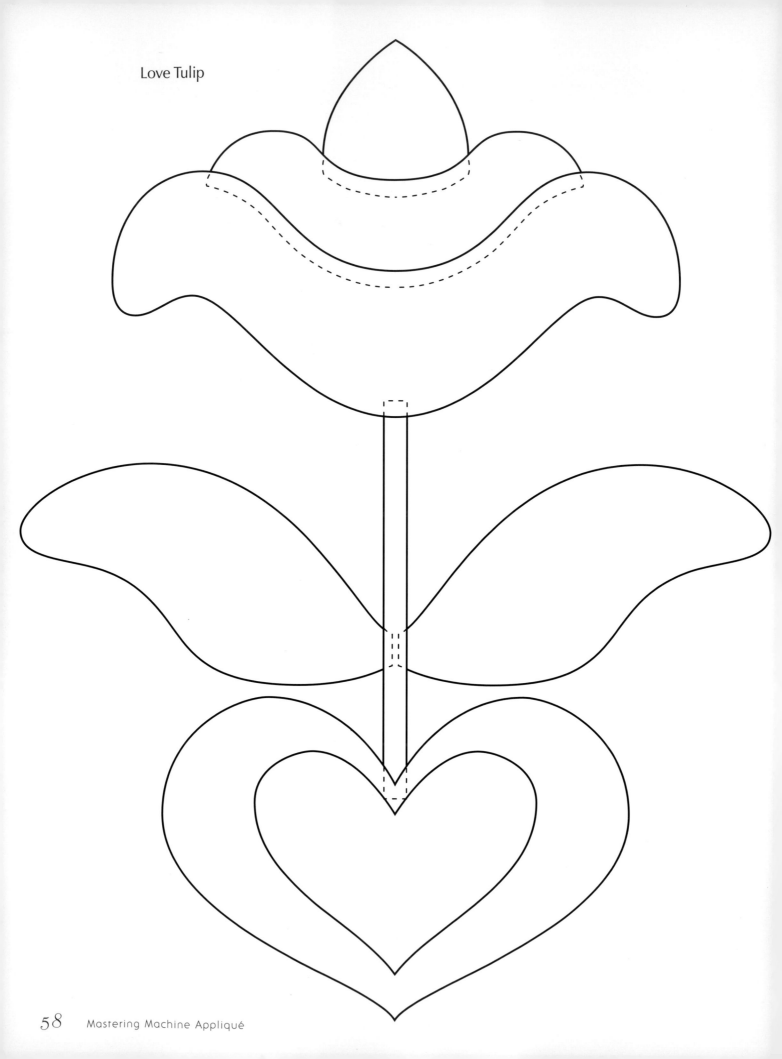

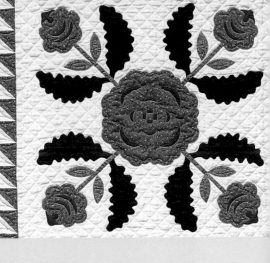

CHAPTER 9

Machine Preparation for Blanket Stitching

Blanket stitch appliqué, also known as Buttonhole stitch, has been used in appliqué throughout history. Blanket-stitching usually refers to a bold, large stitch made with heavy thread. This form was very popular in the early 1900s, especially in the '20s and '30s.

Blanket Stitching

We have all seen Sunbonnet Sue and Dresden Plate quilts appliquéd with heavy black thread, the Blanket stitch securing raw edges to the background fabric. Buttonhole stitching is generally a smaller, tighter stitch, making it less prominent. This stitch is commonly found on Broderie Perse quilts and patterns with intricate designs. The stitching blends into the background or the appliqué piece, and is used simply to secure the edge. It is not meant to be decorative.

The machine preparation and stitch set-up are the same for both types of stitching. The thread size, as well as the stitch width and length, are choices to be made for each project.

Supplies needed:

60/2 cotton embroidery thread for bobbin (white, gray, or black)
30/2 cotton embroidery thread for top—any color
Various threads to experiment with
75/11 Universal needle
Open-toe appliqué foot
Fusing agent
Fabric
Stabilizer

The Stitches

Check your sewing machine manual to see if a Blanket stitch is available on your machine. Mechanical machines are not as apt to have a true Blanket or Buttonhole stitch as are computerized machines. These stitches are often referred to as Hemstitch, Point de Paris, or Pin stitch. The basic element that you are looking for is the structure of the stitch. There is a straight stitch forward, then a zigzag to the left and back again. Some machines have the zigzag stitching to the right. If this is the case on your machine, see if you can mirror image it so that it stitches to the left for ease of handling the fabric. The Blanket stitch is the easiest to control around corners and curves as every part of the stitch is going forward.

True forward motion Blanket stitch

Some machines have two stitches forward and two to the left and back. These stitches do not fill in as well on the edge.

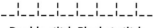
Double stitch Blanket stitch

Other machines will offer a multiple stitch version. They stitch forward, back, forward, left, right, etc. This stitch configuration is more difficult to guide around curves and points.

Multiple-stitch Blanket stitch

You might find that you have an Overlock stitch that appears similar to the Blanket stitch. This stitch has an angled side stitch. This stitch is more limited in use, because creating even stitches around curves and points is difficult if not impossible to do.

Overlock stitch

If you are shopping for a new machine, check the stitch configurations offered and be sure that a true Blanket stitch is available if you think you will be doing this technique. Nothing is more frustrating than to purchase a new machine, only to find you can't do a simple stitch like this.

Setting the Machine Up for Blanket Stitch

Stitch Width and Length

The stitch width and length you select is partly a matter of personal preference, and partly a matter of durability. The relationship of the size of the stitch to the size of the appliqué you are working with, the prominence of the stitch, and the ability of the stitch to secure the edge and prevent raveling must all be taken into consideration.

The longer the distance between the zigzag stitches, the more need there is for a turned edge on the appliqué unit. If the edge is raw, and the stitches are spaced far apart, the edge will not be secured in place

sufficiently and fraying can occur. If you prefer a raw-edge appliqué, you can stitch the raw edge using a tiny zigzag and invisible thread, and then stitch the edge again with the larger Blanket stitch and appropriate thread. This technique eliminates the need for a turned edge, but still has a secure raw edge and the more decorative stitches for appearance.

If the pieces have very tight curves and lots of corners or points, it is easier to work with small, tight Buttonhole stitches. A single thread through a 75/11 needle is needed for these smaller stitches.

Practice with Your Machine

Before practicing the stitch techniques or working on a project, gather up various sizes and types of threads and needles, and play with the machine and the stitches. Experiment with threads to find the ones that create the looks you desire.

I find the fine machine embroidery threads such as Mettler 60/2 and DMC 50/2 too fine and tightly twisted to cover raw edges sufficiently. Sewing weight cotton (50/3) is too thick and stiff for the edge. When I tried 30 weight/2-ply machine embroidery thread I was pleasantly surprised. This thread is thicker than the fine embroidery threads and more softly twisted. When stitched, the twist loosens and fills in the stitch with a fuller look. These are the reasons I prefer this thread for this technique. By experimenting, you too will find which threads give you the look you want on each project. Remember to add the sample you are about to make to your sample notebook, with all the appropriate notes.

Tip *When a heavy-looking stitch is desired, try using two spools of 30/2 thread on the top of your machine. Check your manual for how to properly thread a machine using two spools. The threads are inserted through a size 90/14 topstitching needle. Use 60/2 in the bobbin.*

Comparison of when single and double threads are used as top threads;
a) 2 spools of 30/2 embroidery thread,
b) Renaissance thread, c) Perle cotton rayon, d) Artfloss, e) Cotty, f) Jean Stitch

Start your experimentation by threading the machine with 30 weight, 2-ply cotton embroidery thread and a 75/11 Universal needle. Use a 60/2 thread in the bobbin. Program the single-stitched Blanket stitch (see page 60) into the machine.

Begin by stitching the pre-selected width and length settings of your machine. If any tension adjustments are necessary, make them and make a note of it.

Next, sew lines of stitches varying the stitch width and length. Make a note of each setting as you go.

You might find as you play that you like a certain ratio of the width to the length of the stitch. As a general rule, the stitch length should be equal to or longer than the stitch width. I have found that by keeping the length .5mm longer than the width, I get a very pleasing ratio, and corners and points are easier to handle. You might want to program these into your machine and stitch samples of each. Remember to always make samples of the corners, curves, and points of your actual appliqué pieces before starting any new project. This enables you to find the best ratio for those particular shapes and sizes.

Stitch Ratio	
Length	Width
1.5	1.0
2.0	1.5
2.5	2.0
3.0	2.5
3.5	3.0
4.0	3.5
4.5	4.0
5.0	4.5

Blanket Stitch Tips

When you have worked through various stitch combinations, you are ready to go on to the techniques of curves, points, and corners. Blanket stitching is often thought of as a simple technique, but I have always found it to be a challenging skill and one of the more difficult ones to master. The key is to fit the stitch to the appliqué piece. Keep these ideas in mind when you encounter a difficult situation.

✹ Short and narrow stitches are the easiest to work with, especially when the appliqué shape has tight curves and points.

✹ Create a measuring device by stitching a sample line of stitches the size you choose for your project. If you use this measuring device to mark a few stitches before corners or when you need to join up with the beginning of the stitching line, you will be able to match things up evenly.

✹ An open-toe appliqué foot is a must so you can see each stitch. Learn to train your eye to look at the fabric edge in relationship to the needle instead of using the toe of the foot as the guide.

CHAPTER 10

Blanket Stitch Appliqué Techniques

Blanket stitching generally covers a raw edge finish like Satin stitch appliqué.

Stitching Techniques

Refer to Chapters Four-Six for instructions in preparing your appliqué pieces before you begin to practice the stitch techniques. Note: My favorite method is to remove the stiffness, using the method shown on page 40. If you want to work with a turned edge, refer to Chapter Twelve for methods of edge preparation.

Prepare fabric with the fusing agent and technique of your choice, using the template shapes on page 135-136. Make several of each shape. Again, make a notebook of your samples as you go and record any tricks that you discover, or ideas for counting and measuring that make your work more accurate.

Before you start to practice, there are a few details that need to be discussed.
1. Needle Position – It is easiest to control the needle when you know where the first stitch will be. If your machine has a "pattern begin" or "pattern start" function, engage it. This feature will ensure that you always start at the same point of the stitch—either the zigzag or the straight part. Sew some sample stitches with this function to see where your machine begins the stitch. It is easiest to start the stitching with the straight part of the stitch.

2. Locking the beginning thread tails—There are two ways to lock off the beginning of the stitch. I generally program my machine into the straight stitch mode, bring the bobbin thread to the top, and take two or three tiny short stitches just alongside the appliqué edge (in the ditch). Once this is done, the thread tails can be cut off. You can also leave long tails that can be knotted by hand later.

3. Locking stitches at the end–The most effective way I have found to secure the thread tails at the end is to stop on the last zigzag stitch. Then I program my machine to take a 3-step zigzag stitch (this is the stitch that takes three tiny stitches in each zig and each zag). The width is set to the same width as the Blanket stitch, but the length is 0. Let the needle zig, then zag. The tiny stitches are locked in tight, and do not show at all!

4. Stitch Placement–The straight stitch part of the stitch should be as close to the cut edge of the appliqué as possible. The needle will rub the cut edge, but be careful that it doesn't fall on the top of the edge. The zigzag part of the stitch is totally on the appliqué. Stitch slowly.

The Stitches

Outside Corners using Shapes #1 and #3

Outside and inside corners are the easiest to stitch. Start with the template of the box, stitching the outside edges.

1. Start on one side, in the center, lock off stitches, or make sure you have long enough tails to tie off later.

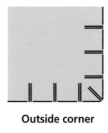

Outside corner

2. Begin stitching, carefully guiding the needle so that it touches the edge of the appliqué, and the zigzag is totally on the top of the appliqué piece.

3. As you approach the corner, you are going to work at keeping consistent spacing between all the zigzag stitches along the point of the corner, as well as on the side.

4. The last stitch you take is the straight stitch. If you have chosen the correct ratio of stitch width and length, the last straight stitch will end exactly at the point.

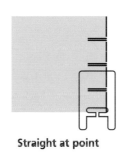

Straight at point

5. Next, lift the presser foot, and pivot the appliqué so that the next zigzag stitch will form the diagonal of the point (45° counterclockwise). Make both of the zigzag stitches (left, then back to right, all in the same holes). Lower the needle into the hole on the right swing.

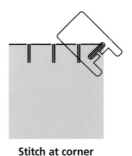

Stitch at corner

6. Lift the presser foot again, pivoting the appliqué so that the foot is aligned with the new straight edge. The next stitch will go forward.

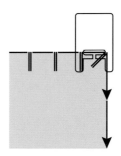

Turning the corner

Check to see that the zigzags on both sides of the corner do not overlap. They can be close together, and even touch. Overlapping indicates that the stitch width is too wide or the length is too short.

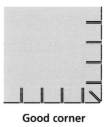

Good corner

Stitches too wide

Inside Corners Using Shapes #2 and #3

You may find inside corners a bit easier than outside corners. They are less obvious if they are not perfectly spaced.

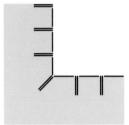

Inside corner

1. Stitch on the straight edge, approaching an inside corner. Try to keep the spacing as consistent as you can. End with the straight stitch.

Last stitch at corner

2. With the needle in the down position, pivot the fabric (45° clockwise) so the needle will swing into the fabric on the next stitch. Make both of the stitches (left and right) of the zigzag. Stop with the needle in the right swing and in the same hole.

Turning the corner

3. Pivot the fabric and align the foot with the next straight edge. The first stitch will move forward on the straight part of the stitch. Stitch toward the next inside corner and repeat.

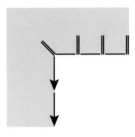

Final turn at corner

When you have mastered the basics, cut out and fuse fabric using Shape #3 and practice some more.

Another way I like to stitch inside corners is to make several stitches in the corner, which is easily achieved by dropping the feed dogs.

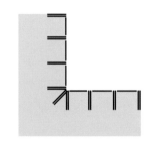

Starburst corner made with feed dogs down

1. Allow the first set of zigzag stitches taken at the corner to be perpendicular to the cut edge.

First step of corner zigzag

2. Once the first set of zigzag stitches are taken, pivot the fabric 45° with the needle in the hole at the corner. Take the next zigzag stitch. Notice that the machine needs to make an extra stitch in the hole first. (This would be the forward stitch if the feed dogs were up.) When the zigzag stitch is completed, take one more stitch in the corner hole (again, this would have been the forward stitch if the feed dogs were in the up position).

Second step of corner

3. Pivot 45° again. Take another set of zigzag stitches.

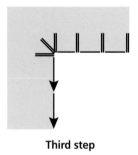

Third step

4. You should see a perfect little starburst in the inside corner if the stitches have been placed correctly. Now put your feed dogs up and allow the machine to take the next stitch forward, and continue.

Inside and Outside Curves Using Shapes #5 and #6

I've always thought curves were easier than corners and points. The trick is to keep all the stitches perfectly perpendicular to the cut edge of the appliqué piece at all times. This requires constant pivoting of the fabric, but never turning the fabric as you are sewing. If you turn as you sew, the straight part of the stitch will not be aligned exactly with the edge of the appliqué.

1. Start stitching on the part of the line that is the straightest. As you approach an outside curve, remember that you pivot only after you have taken the straight part of the stitch.

2. With the needle in the down position, lift the presser foot and pivot the appliqué. Be sure that the zigzag stitches angle toward the center point of the curve. You may find that outside curve stitches appear closer together.

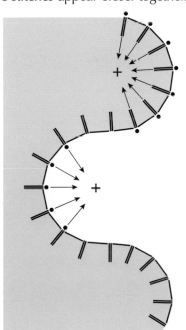

Pivot points and angles

3. Now you will approach the inside curve. Pivot only on the straight stitch section of the stitch. Again, the zigzag stitches need to angle toward the center of the curve. These stitches should have the look of fanning out.

Sharp Outside Points Using Shapes #7 and #8

Sharp points are the most difficult of all the aspects of Blanket stitching. The wider the stitch width, the more difficult it is to maneuver these points. Very sharp points are best left to other techniques.

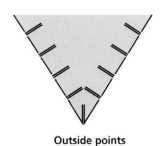

Outside points

You will use the same basic techniques as used for corners, but it is critical that the stitches on the sides of the points be accurately positioned. When you look at a correctly stitched point, you should see that the last zigzag stitches before the point meet at an imaginary dividing line down the center of the point. These stitches cannot cross that line.

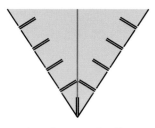

Imaginary center line

If the forward stitch places the last set of zigzag stitches too close to the point, the last zigzag stitches will overlap.

Crossed zigzag stitches

Notice that the length of the straight stitch between the last zigzag stitch and the point is longer than the distance between the other straight stitches. This is achieved by lifting the presser foot and carefully moving the fabric forward so that the next stitch will be in the proper position.

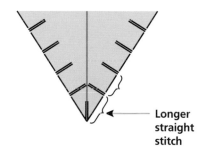

Longer straight stitch

Let's practice this step by step.

1. Stitch forward until you come to the position of the last zigzag before the point. Complete the last zigzag. Stop with the needle in the fabric as the right-hand swing stitch is completed.

2. Turn the hand wheel to begin the next stitch, which will be the straight stitch forward. Just before the needle goes back into the fabric, stop. Lift the presser foot and move the fabric so the needle is exactly on the point of the appliqué fabric.

3. Lower the needle into the fabric at the correct position.

4. Pivot the fabric so that the next stitch—the zigzag— will be directly on the point. Make the zigzag stitches.

5. When the needle is back in the right-hand swing, it should enter the same hole it has been in. The fabric has not moved forward at this point.

6. Lift the presser foot and pivot the fabric so the foot is aligned with the next side of the point. Again manually take the next stitch with the hand wheel. When the needle is in the up position, move the fabric the same distance as you did on the first side. Lower the needle and presser foot and continue stitching.

Remember that these points take practice and patience. The more you do them, the better you will be able to see the distances and your accuracy will improve.

Sharp Inside Points Using Shapes #7 and #8

You get a reward for persevering through the outside points! Inside points are handled just like inside corners. You may occasionally need to manually make a slightly longer stitch to get exactly into the point, but it is not as critical as outside points. Try the starburst point too.

Inside point

Pattern Preparation for Invisible Machine Appliqué

Whereas Satin stitch and Blanket stitch appliqué are raw-edge techniques, Invisible Machine appliqué utilizes a turned edge. This requires completely different methods of preparation. Instead of fusibles, freezer paper and templates are used. The preparation time is greater, but the stitching is faster and easier. The methods in this section will teach you how to create machine appliqués that emulate the look of fine hand appliqué.

When choosing a design for Invisible machine appliqué, there are a few things to be considered before the patterns and templates are made. Analyzing the design for symmetry will help you decide how the pattern pieces need to be traced. This chapter will address symmetrical or asymmetrical design issues, the lack of seam allowances, and whether or not grainline considerations and the pattern's complexity affect the choice of template methods.

The basic preparation of pattern pieces for the machine appliqué techniques presented here are very similar to those used for hand appliqué. In fact, you will find these methods very useful for hand stitching. There are as many ways to prepare for stitching as there are stitchers. I have only presented here the ones that seem to be tried-and-true in my classes. Don't hesitate to adapt any of these techniques to other methods that you may already use. Remember, if it works, it's right!

Pattern Images

Symmetrical and Mirror Image Designs

Before making templates using any of the methods described in Chapter Twelve, design orientation needs to analyzed. Whether a design is symmetrical, asymmetrical, or mirrored will affect the way the pattern units are traced.

Symmetrical designs are identical on either side of the center. If you place a mirror down the exact center of the design lengthwise, the mirror will reflect the exact image on the other side. Or if placed in the center crosswise, the tops and bottoms will match. The pattern below shows a design that is totally symmetrical. All the pattern pieces are identical from side to side and top to bottom. They are traced from the top of the pattern as you see them. You do not need to create a reverse image of anything, since no matter where the pattern pieces are placed on the design, they will fit.

Symmetrical design

You will often find that appliqué designs are symmetrical in their layout and all the shapes are the same, but certain pieces need to be reversed to fit properly within the design. These are known as mirror image designs. In the following design, both of the birds are the same, the body and wing pieces are identical, but they face in opposite directions.

Mirror image design

When tracing onto the freezer paper, one bird needs to be traced with the pattern or tagboard templates facing up, and the other needs to be traced in "reverse image." To do this, simply turn the pattern over and trace from the wrong side of the pattern, or turn the templates over and trace from the backside.

Some designs are totally asymmetrical, as the design below shows. This is a design that needs to be traced entirely reverse image. If this isn't done, the design will look opposite the original design when the appliqué pieces are laid out.

Asymmetrical design

Tracing

Patterns and templates for Invisible Machine appliqué are the exact size of the finished piece, with no seam allowance added. When tracing the pattern to make the templates, you need to break apart the elements of the design. Do not trace the entire design as one unit and then try to cut it apart. It is difficult to keep perfect cut edges on both sides of a line. Separate each unit of the design and draw it separately. DO NOT ADD ANY SEAM ALLOWANCES.

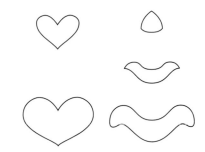

Pattern pieces broken up and separated

When making the pattern units for invisible appliqué, the importance of accuracy and precision cannot be overemphasized. The quality of the finished project is contingent on this precision. Trace your pattern pieces as carefully as you can. If tracing a line is difficult for you, make tagboard or plastic templates to trace around. This reduces the amount of free-hand tracing.

Templates

Read through the methods presented here and try each one before deciding which one best adapts to your particular project and working style. Eventually you will use all the techniques because they are adapted to specific problem areas in working with appliqué pieces.

Hard Templates for Tracing

When multiples of the same pattern piece are needed, it is often easier to make a hard template. Tagboard, manila file folders, index cards, template material, and various other products can be used to make hard templates. This firmer material is used because the edges

remain crisp after drawing around them over and over. Tracing around a template is more accurate than tracing the pattern pieces individually several times. Identify each unit that makes up the design; you will need a template for each shape.

Various template materials

I like to use freezer paper to trace the pattern onto first. It is easy to see through, and will iron onto the template material.

1. Trace each different pattern shape onto the paper side (the rough side) of the freezer paper with a pencil. Do not add seam allowances at this time; trace only the shape that will be the finished appliqué.

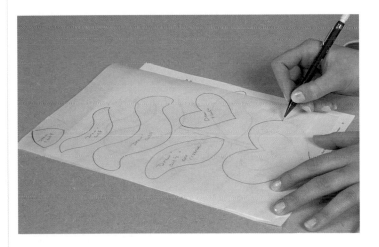

2. Do not cut the pattern out, but press the freezer paper onto a piece of tagboard.

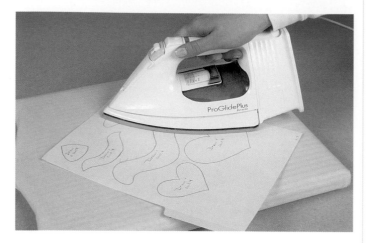

3. Now very carefully and accurately cut out the tagboard piece on the line.

4. Mark "front" on the freezer paper as a reminder. This is important when you have pattern units that need to be traced both face up and reverse image.

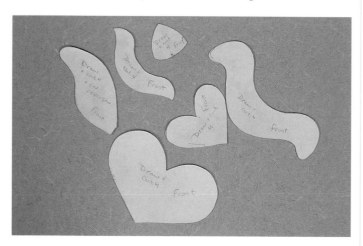

Once the templates are made, they can be used to trace the shapes onto freezer paper for the pattern that is used for each appliqué, or used to work edges over when not using freezer paper. These techniques will be discussed in Chapter Twelve.

Freezer Paper Templates

While hard templates are used to trace around or iron edges over, freezer paper templates are pressed directly onto the fabric. If you do not have multiples of the same units to work with or you do not care to make permanent templates from tagboard, you can simply trace each unit directly onto the freezer paper. You will need a separate freezer paper template for each unit in the design.

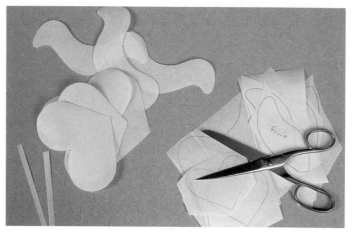

If you dislike the idea of tracing each and every piece for the project, consider printing the pattern units onto freezer paper with a photocopy machine. Photocopy machines can save a lot of time in this tedious stage of preparation. If you have one available to you, refer to Chapter Twenty for complete instructions.

Marking

Identify and mark any edges that act as seam allowances or extensions and will not be turned under, such as the ends of a stem or the inside curves of petals that a center sits on top of. These are extensions that are needed to rebuild the design. Mark the pattern with "Xs" for each extension.

Xs marked for non-turned edges

Grainline

Paying attention to the grainline will make working with certain shapes easier, and the finished product look nicer. To determine grainline, pull on a piece of fabric. The direction that is parallel to the selvage is called lengthwise grain. This direction has the least amount of stretch. If you pull on the fabric selvage-to-selvage, you will be testing the crosswise grain. You will find there is a bit more stretch this direction than lengthwise. When you pull diagonally, you are stretching bias. This is the direction of the most stretch.

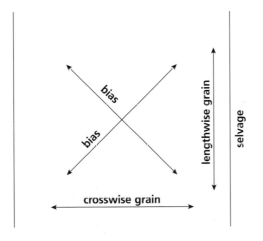

Grainlines

There are no particular grainline rules for placement of appliqué pieces, especially if the pieces are small and there will be quilting stitches on the surface of the appliqué. However, here are some tips that can make a difference.

If the pieces are large or if no quilting will be on their surface, consider matching the grainline of the appliqué to the grainline of the background fabric.

Appliqué grainlines match grainlines of background

Grainline can also affect the ease of turning the edges over. You will find that bias is easier to turn under than are straight-grain edges. For this reason it is helpful to place the pattern shapes with their longest part along the bias of the fabric. Curves are also easier to manipulate when on the bias.

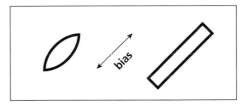

Edge placement on bias

When you have the pattern analyzed and the templates made, you are ready to prepare the fabric appliqué pieces. Read through Chapter Twelve and try each of the techniques. You will find each of them has its merits, and you might prefer one method for one project and a different method for a different project.

CHAPTER 12

Preparing Appliqué Pieces

Once the pattern shapes have been made into templates, or freezer paper templates have been cut for each piece, you are ready to select a method for turning the seam allowance over the edge of the template. This chapter will cover several methods for turning edges. I recommend that you take the time to try all of them, and choose the one that works best for you. You will find that different methods can have various uses, so no one method is the best for all applications.

Preparing Appliqué Pieces

Method #1—Glued Edges Over Freezer Paper

This method uses a glue stick to secure the seam allowances. It gives a very secure edge to place the presser foot against.

▼ **NOTE: When using this method, the background fabric will need to be cut away from behind the appliqué in order to remove the paper.**

1. Trace each unit needed for the design onto the rough side of the freezer paper. Review the information about reverse image patterns on page 68 if you are using an asymmetrical or mirror image design. You need a freezer paper pattern for each unit of the design.

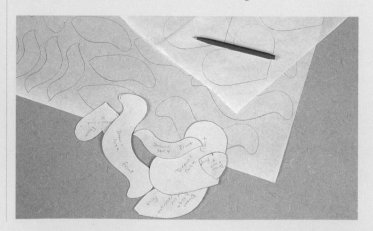

2. Cut out each pattern piece, being very careful that the cut edges are as smooth and even as possible.

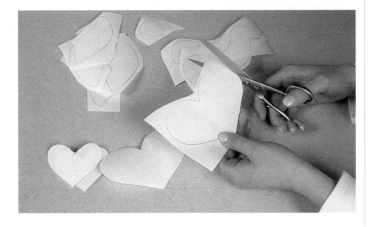

3. Next, choose your fabrics. Refer to the information on grainlines on page 71 before applying freezer paper to the fabric. Place the fabric wrong side up on your ironing board.

Tip *If your ironing board is heavily padded, you might find that a hard surface like a wood cutting board or piece of heavy cardboard allows the freezer paper to adhere more easily. Place the freezer paper templates plastic side down on the wrong side of the fabric. Leave 1/2" between each paper piece. Check grainline placement if needed.*

4. Using a hot dry iron (cotton or linen setting), press the paper onto the fabric, being careful not to scorch the paper or the fabric. Scorching makes removal of the paper difficult, and it could damage your fabric. Be sure that the paper adheres firmly. If the pattern edges release, press firmly again.

5. With very sharp scissors, begin cutting around the shapes, adding 3/16" seam allowance on all sides of the paper. Be careful not to let the seam allowance grow to 1/4", because an extension this wide makes it difficult to turn the edge smoothly and evenly.

A 3/16" seam allowance eliminates the tucks and points on the edge as well as a lot of clipping that can later cause fraying of the appliqué edge.

6. Before turning the edges under, look at the pattern pieces and identify inside curves and points that need to be clipped, see page 90.

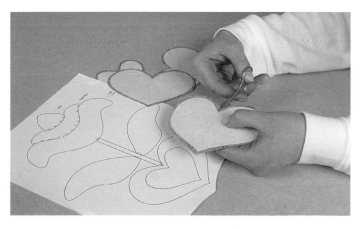

7. Using a fresh fabric-basting glue stick, apply a coating of glue to the seam allowance as well as to the width of the seam allowance on the freezer paper.

8. Following the guidelines on page 115 on turning smooth edges, points, and corners, carefully roll the edges over to the paper side, using tiny pinch and twist motions with the tip of your thumb and forefinger.

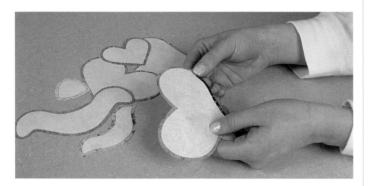

9. Turn the piece over and examine the edges. They should be smooth and perfect. Any unevenness or waviness along the edges is the result of poor paper cutting or bending the paper over with the seam allowance. A lighter touch will prevent this. Now the pieces are ready for placement.

10. When you have finished stitching the appliqué pieces to the background, remove the paper. To do this, turn the project over and cut the background fabric 1/4" inside the stitching of all the stitched pieces.

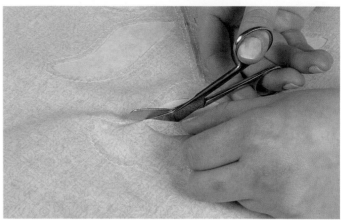

11. Dampen the glued seam allowance with water. A spray bottle works well for this. Carefully remove the freezer paper.

Method #2—Ironed Edges over Freezer Paper

This method eliminates the need for the glue stick. You press the edges over the paper edge and secure them by pressing them to the plastic side of the freezer paper. This method also eliminates the need to cut out the backing because the paper is removed before the design is completely stitched around. Do be careful when working with your fingers so close to a hot iron. The Clover Mini Iron might be a good choice here. Also watch that the delicate paper edge does not get bent over while pressing.

Begin by reviewing the information on symmetrical designs and reverse image tracing on page 68. Make sure you understand how the position of the freezer paper on the fabric affects the final product. Because the plastic side of the paper faces up (not down), you will need to adjust your pattern directions. Prepare and trace the required shapes onto freezer paper, one piece for each unit in the design.

1. Place the freezer paper onto the wrong side of the fabric, plastic side facing you, leaving ½" between each pattern piece. Pin securely in place.

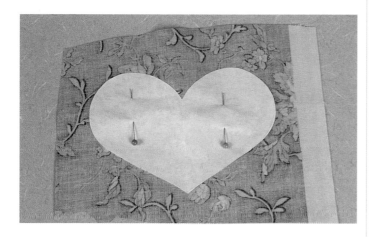

2. Cut around each pattern, leaving a ³/₁₆" seam allowance.

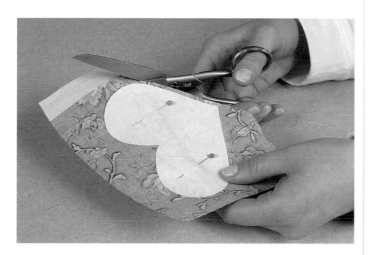

3. Using the guidelines on page 115, clip the necessary curves and points.

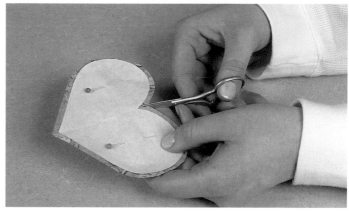

4. Using a hot dry iron, carefully ease the seam allowance over the edge of the freezer paper and press onto the plastic coating with the tip of the iron. This is where a small-pointed travel iron or mini-iron is very helpful.

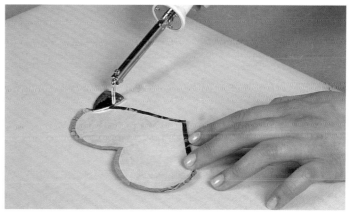

5. Stitch around the unit. Stop 2" before you come to where the stitching began. Remove the paper by pulling it out of this opening. Because glue hasn't been used, the paper comes out easily. After the paper is removed, complete the stitching.

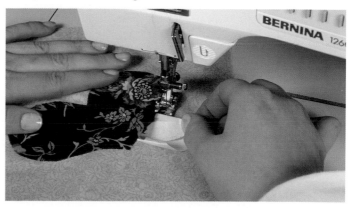

Method #3—Freezer Paper on Top of Fabric

A third method is to apply the freezer paper to the right side of the fabric. Elly Sienkiewicz developed this technique for Baltimore-style appliqué. It is especially helpful where multiple layers are needed. By having the freezer paper on top, the paper can be removed right after the stitching is completed, without working from the back. It is trickier, however, to get smooth, even edges with this method.

1. Iron freezer paper pieces onto the RIGHT side of the fabric, leaving ½" space between each pattern piece.

2. Cut out each piece, adding ³/₁₆" seam allowance around all edges of the paper. Clip where necessary.

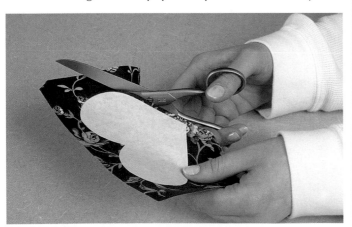

3. Using a fresh glue stick, apply a film of glue on the wrong side of the seam allowance. Carefully roll the seam allowance over to the wrong side of the fabric. There will not be a paper edge to roll over this time. The paper is used as a guideline only. Take your time, and work with very small bits of fabric at a time, since this edge is harder to achieve without the paper inside.

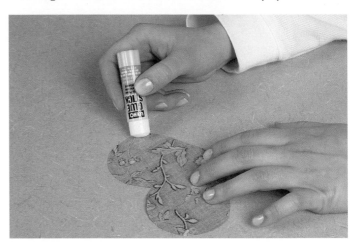

4. Leave the paper on until the piece is stitched in place.

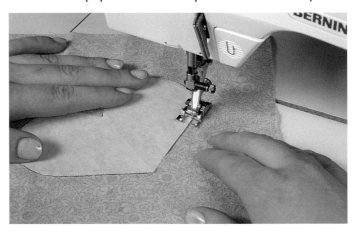

5. Then, the paper is easily removed from the top side.

Method #4—Templar or Tagboard Templates

Templates eliminate the need to trace individual pattern pieces onto freezer paper. Also, you will have no paper to remove.

1. Trace the shape of each template onto the wrong side of your chosen fabric.

2. Cut ³/16" to ¹/4" beyond the drawn line for seam allowances. (Because you will be working with an iron instead of your fingers and glue, the seam allowance may need to be wider than ³/16" for ease in manipulation.)

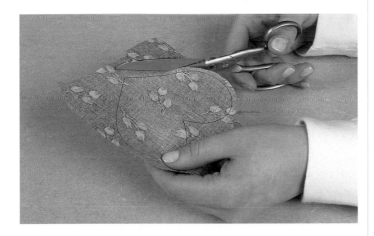

3. Clip any necessary curves and points, then identify the edges that will not be pressed over.

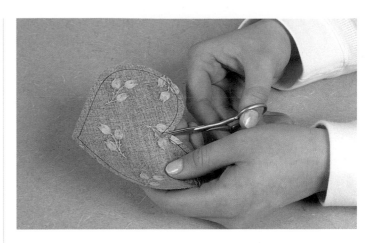

4. Spray a little spray starch or fabric stiffener into a small dish or the cap of the can. Place the appliqué piece wrong side up on the ironing board. Using your fingertip or a small paintbrush, dampen the appliqué shape with starch along the seam allowance area.

5. Lay the template on the fabric, aligning the drawn line with the cut edge of the template.

6. Using the side of the tip of a hot dry iron, ease the seam allowance over the template edge and press. Hold the iron on the seam allowance until the starch dries. The starch helps the edge become crisp and stay in place. Roll all edges over and press securely in the same manner.

7. Carefully remove the template and press again from the right side of the appliqué. The spray starch helps stiffen the edge so that the paper is not missed as a stabilizer when stitching.

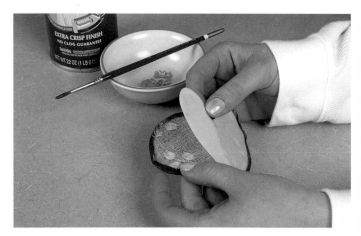

Method #5—Using a Facing of Wash-Away or Heat-Away Products

This method works nicely for larger, simple shapes. I would not recommend it if there are tight curves in the pattern. The quality of the edge depends on your ability to sew perfectly on the line, and trim and turn exactly on the sewn line.

Solvy, Sol-u-web, RinsAway, and Heat-away are excellent products for this method. The bulk of another piece of fabric is eliminated completely, as these products will disappear with water or heat. Review page 24 for more information on stabilizers.

1. Trace the desired designs onto the stabilizer of your choice. Do not add extensions or seam allowances. Use a pencil, Pigma pen, or water-erasable marker for tracing. Leave 1/2" allowance around the line you trace.

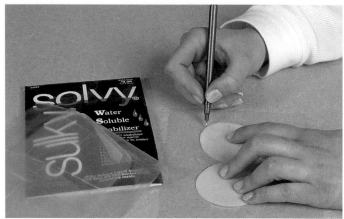

2. Place the stabilizer shapes on the right side of the appliqué fabric and pin in place. With small stitches (12-14 stitches per inch), machine straight-stitch on the drawn line. The small stitches will help you get smooth curves.

3. Cut a 3/16" seam allowance beyond the stitched line. Clip curves and inside points. Blunt-cut any outside corners and points.

Tip   *Pinking shears are helpful at this stage. They help reduce the bulk from the seam allowance and eliminate the possibility of a ridge showing where the seam allowances are turned in.*

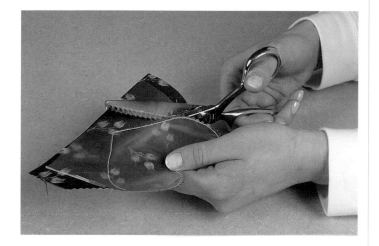

4. Make a slit with the sharp point of small scissors across the middle of the stablizer.
Carefully turn the piece right side out, and finger-press the seam to smooth it and make it lie flat.

Tip   *When turning right side out, a blunt object like a point turner, knitting needle or chopstick is helpful for pushing out and smoothing the edges.*

5. If pressing is necessary, use only a dry iron on the fabric side of the wash-away products. Do not iron heat-away products.

Attach appliqué to the background fabric and stitch in place. Remove the water-soluble products by submerging in cold water, or use an iron to remove the heat-away products.

CHAPTER 13

Building the Design

Once the pattern units are cut out, they are ready to be laid out into the design. One trick that I find really speeds up the stitching process is to pre-stitch units together before putting everything onto the background fabric. For example, in the Love Tulip pattern, we can combine the flower units as well as the two hearts before applying them to the background.

1. The first step is going to sound incorrect, but trust me and do it anyway. Lay the bud of the Love Tulip pattern down, right side up. Apply glue from a glue stick onto the seam allowance extension at the bottom of the bud. You will be applying it to the right side of the piece, not the paper side.

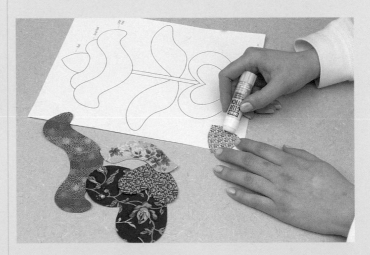

2. Using the pattern as a guide, position the bud on the pattern. The glued seam allowance is now ready to have the small petal put on top of it. Stick the two together.

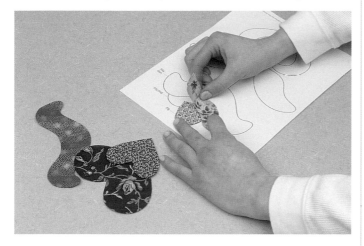

3. Continue by applying glue to the seam allowance of the small petal (right side again). Position the large petal on top of the small petal, and stick them together.

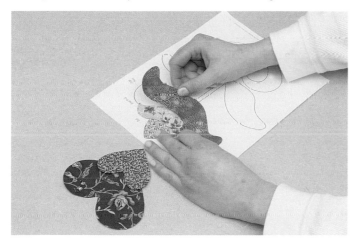

Now the flower unit is joined. Invisible Machine appliqué each of the units to each other. Once they are stitched together, the entire flower can be placed on the background. When the entire flower is assembled and you are stitching, you will go around the perimeter of the entire flower, instead of stopping and starting for each individual piece. This prevents excessive manipulation of the background fabric, and offers a better chance to have continuous stitching.

The hearts can also be joined, but with a slightly different technique.

1. Turn the small heart over to the wrong side. Very carefully apply glue from a glue stick or Glue BasteIt to the seam allowance only. Try to avoid getting glue on the paper.

2. Carefully position the small heart onto the right side of the large heart. Since you can't see the pattern through the large heart, use your eye for centering the small heart. Paper will be removed from BOTH hearts later.

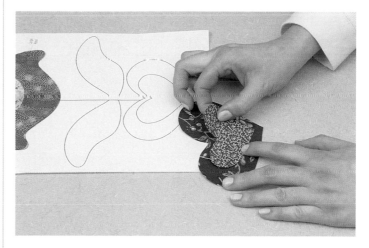

For more complicated patterns, like Baltimore quilt blocks, the use of transparency film is very helpful.

1. Copy the pattern onto transparency film (acetate). Be sure to buy the type appropriate for your copy machine.

2. Starting with the bottom-most units, apply glue to the seam allowance extensions. Start building the appliqué upwards, gluing the pieces together as you go. Use the transparent pattern to check placement as the layers are built.

3. Stitch each of the pieces to one another. Once the unit is stitched together, it is ready to be placed on the background fabric.

This technique of using transparency film for placement is excellent anytime you have multiple layers and can no longer see the pattern from underneath the background fabric.

Building the Design

Once all the appliqué pieces are prepared, you are ready to build the design onto the background fabric. If you can't see through the background fabric well enough to see the lines of the pattern underneath, a lightbox is helpful. This is especially helpful when working with dark fabrics. I do not recommend drawing the placement lines onto the background fabric. Through the cutting and preparation stages, the pattern pieces are apt to change shape slightly and probably won't match the drawn lines exactly. The lightbox allows you to place the fabric on top of the pattern and see through the fabric for placement.

1. Prepare the background fabric by folding it into fourths (b & c), or any number of divisions needed, and press LIGHTLY with an iron. It is often helpful to also press in the diagonal centers (d & e). These lines are known as registration lines.

a.

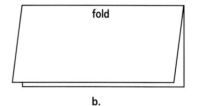

b.   c.

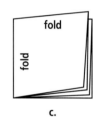

d.

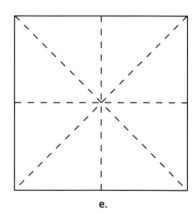

e.

Folding fabrics
a. Square
b. Folded in half
c. Folded in fourths
d. Fourths folded diagonally
e. Unfolded square showing crease lines

2. If your pattern is in sections, you should prepare a full-scale layout of the finished design to use for placement. Mark the centering registration lines on the pattern to be used to line up with the background fabric.

3. Position the background fabric over the layout pattern, matching the registration lines, and tape or pin in place. Use a lightbox if needed.

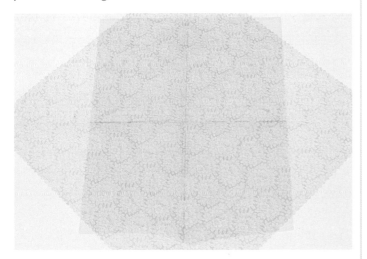

4. Starting with the bottom-most units, begin placing and pinning (or use Roxanne's Glue Baste It or a glue stick if you prefer) each pattern piece to the background fabric. Using very thin pins (like the Iris silk pins or the shorter Clover appliqué pins), pin along the edges. Place the pins perpendicular to the edge to make them easy to remove while stitching. Pin about every $3/4$" on each piece to prevent it from slipping or pivoting while stitching.

Once the design is placed and secured, you can begin stitching. Unlike hand appliqué, with machine work, the technique of placing one piece at a time and stitching it down before placing another is not advisable. If anything should slip from the pressure of the presser foot, it would not be noticeable until another piece is ready to be positioned. The Invisible Machine appliqué techniques we are using are very difficult (if not impossible) to remove, making this risky.

CHAPTER 14

Machine Preparation for Invisible Machine Appliqué

Invisible Machine appliqué provides instant gratification. The preparation of the pattern units is the most time-consuming part of the process. Once your pieces are ready to stitch, the hard work is finished. You will be amazed at how fast you can stitch your appliqués, and how much your machine stitching will resemble the finest handwork.

Machine Set-Up

Start with a thoroughly cleaned and oiled machine. If it hasn't been to the repairman for awhile, take it in and have it cleaned, oiled, and adjusted.

Begin by threading the machine. The bobbin must be wound with 60 weight/2-ply fine machine embroidery thread. Make sure that the thread winds tightly and evenly onto the bobbin. Thread the invisible nylon on the top of the machine. Review Chapters One and Two if you have questions about threads or needles. Use a size 60/8 needle. This is the smallest sewing machine needle available. We use such a small needle to enable us to get as close to the edge of the appliqué as possible. The larger the needle, the more distance there is from the eye to the side of the blade. This puts the stitches farther away from the edge of the appliqué. Because the 60/8 is so fine, the needle eye is very close to the edge of the needle, allowing the stitches to be as close as possible to the edge of the appliqué.

For Invisible Machine appliqué use the Blind stitch which is often used for hems. With some minor adjustments, this stitch can be used to duplicate the look of hand-Blind stitching. Begin by locating the Blind stitch on your stitch selector dial or panel: it forms 4-7 straight stitches, then zigzags to the left. It is important that the stitch makes straight stitches between the zigzags. Some machines only have a stretch-Blind stitch. This stitch has tiny zigzags between the wider zigzags, so it does not have a clean appearance when used for appliqué.

You might find that your machine has another stitch that works even better than the Blind stitch. My Bernina® has a stitch called a Vari-overlock stitch. It has only two stitches between the zigzags and gives a much nicer finished look, as well as needing fewer tension adjustments. The stitch zigzags to the right, but by using the mirror image feature, I can flip it over to the left. Read your machine manual to see what features your machine has to help you make the best stitch possible. For basic settings of different machines, refer to the list on page 86.

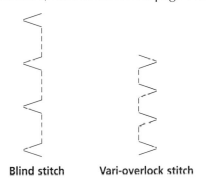

Blind stitch   Vari-overlock stitch

If you cannot get a satisfactory Blind stitch, use a Blanket stitch setting instead. I prefer the Blind stitch because the "v" of the stitch becomes invisible, where the bar of the blanket stitch is two stitches together, and more noticeable. In any event , you want the smallest, most invisible stitch your machine will make, regardless of the type of stitch it is.

 NOTE: If your machine does not have a Blind stitch, or the width of the stitch is not adjustable, you may want to experiment with using a darning foot and working free motion. Set the machine for a Straight stitch instead of a Blind stitch, and the feed dogs are disengaged. Manually create the stitch needed by taking two stitches forward close to the folded edge, and then move the fabric sideways for the tiny zigzag needed to secure the appliqué. Once the zigzag is made, another two stitches forward are made, then one sideways. This eliminates the need to pivot and turn the fabric, making complicated pieces or large bulky, quilt tops much more manageable. However, you will need to practice quite a bit to obtain the control needed to achieve accurate stitching.

Many machines automatically put the needle in the right-hand position when set to Blind stitch. If this is the case, leave it there. The machine will make a nicer stitch in this position.

Now, fine-tune the machine so that this stitch becomes an appliqué stitch instead of a hemming stitch. Begin by sewing a line of these stitches on a scrap of fabric. Notice how far apart they are and how wide the zigzag bite is. Reduce the stitch width to a little narrower than "1". The stitch width should be just wide enough to barely catch 2 to 3 threads of the appliqué fabric. A stitch that is too wide will show and thus spoil the effect, and one that is too narrow will not hold the appliqué in place.

Next, adjust the stitch length. It will be a bit shorter than "1" on most machines, or approximately 25 to 30 stitches to the inch. The distance between the stitches needs to be ⅛"

or slightly shorter. If too much space is left between the stitches, there will be gaps along the edge of the appliqué.

The tension will need to be adjusted because of the extremely short stitch length being used. Start by reducing the top tension slightly. If further adjustments need to be made, refer to page 30 for detailed information on tension adjustments.

It is not unusual to need to tighten the bobbin tension. You may also have to loosen the top slightly to keep the bobbin thread from showing on the top. If you plan to do a lot of this type of sewing, consider purchasing another bobbin case and keeping it tight, using the other case for normal sewing. Test the stitches again, and make sure that NO bobbin thread is showing on the top of the piece.

Tip If you are using a Bernina with an oscillating hook or a Viking 1+, be sure to thread the bobbin thread through the hole in the finger of the bobbin case. This will automatically tighten your bobbin tension. You may need to add additional tension to this setup, but this is the basic starting point for Berninas and the Viking 1+ when doing any type of appliqué.

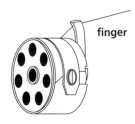
finger

Threading the finger on the bobbin case

If you cannot adjust your bobbin tension, or there seems to be nothing you can do to prevent the bobbin thread from showing, matching the bobbin thread in size 60 weight/2-ply to the background fabric will help alleviate the problem.

Put the open-toe appliqué foot on the machine. This foot allows you to see the stitches clearly as they are being made. Learn to guide by looking at the needle instead of working with the toes of the feet. This is critical when turning curves and corners, and especially points.

Practice this tiny stitch on samples before attempting to stitch your project. You need to train your eyes to do the close work of keeping the needle exactly off the edge of the appliqué, making sure that the zigzag catches the appliqué with every bite.

Basic Machine Settings for Invisible Machine Appliqué

It would be impossible to list the settings of every sewing machine available. The majority of machines have very simple settings, and it is easy enough to figure out your machine with the instructions given above. This list represents the machines I encounter consistently in classrooms all over the country. If yours is not listed here, don't hesitate to go to your dealer for guidance.

Bernina
Model 830
Stitch #1
Width – 1
Length – 1

Models 801, 910, 930
Stitch #2
Width – 1
Length – 1

Model 1000
Stitch #3
Width – 1
Length – 1

Models 1010, 1020, 1030
Stitch #4
Width – 1
Length – 1

Models 1130, 1230, 1260, 1080, 1090
Stitch #4
Mirror Image
Move needle position from far right to center right
Length – 1
Width – 1

Models 1530, 1630
Menu #1
Stitch #3
Mirror Image
Move needle position to center right
Length – 1
Width – 1

Models 130, 140, 150
Stitch #3
Mirror Image
Length – 1
Width – 1

Models 160, 170, 180
NOTE: these machines have a quilting program with Mock Appliqué stitch preprogrammed. However, the stitch has too many stitches between the zigzags to look good, so I personally program the machine using the Vari-overlock stitch.
Stitch #3
Mirror image
Center right needle position
Length – 1
Width –1

New Home
Model 7500
Blind Stitch #41
Pattern turnover
Width – 1.5
Length – .7
Tension – 4
The bulk of the fabric will be on the right with this stitch.

Model 8000
Stitch #16
Width – 0.5
Length – 2.5

Model 9000
Stitch #6
Width – 0.5
Length – 2.5

Models 3000, 4000
Stitch #13
Width – 1.0
Length – 1.0

NOTE: The New Home models 8000 and up will not allow the Blind stitch to be narrower than 2, so the Super Stretch stitch in the set-ups above is the nicest looking stitch available. It is a bit tricky at first around curves and points, but with practice you can achieve a lovely appliqué.

Pfaff

MODEL 1471, 1473
Select a memory bank (P memory)

	Boo	Loo
1	20	0
2	20	4
3	20	8
4	20	12
5	14	16

MODEL 1475
Stitch #16
Length – 0.5
Width – 3.0 – 3.5
Activate double needle button

MODEL 7550, 7570
Stitch #4
Length – 0.5
Width – 3.0 or 3.5
Activate double needle button

MODELS 2030, 2040
Stitch #15
Length – 2.0
Width – 1.0

MODEL 6122
Stitch #H or K
Width – 1.0
Length – 1.5 – 2.0

Viking

MODEL 500, ROSE, LILY
Stitch #33
Width – 1.0
Length – 2.0

MODEL 1100, #1, 1+
Stitch #30
Length – 0.2
Width – 1.0

DESIGNER I
Stitch A25
Width – 1
Length – 0.2
Tension – 2.4

Disclaimer: These are basic starting settings. They may not be exactly where you will end up, but program your machine starting here, then fine-tune as you make samples and adjust tensions.

CHAPTER 15

Invisible Machine Appliqué Techniques

To understand the needle placement for the Invisible Machine stitch, fold a piece of fabric and place this fold on another piece of fabric, or use an actual appliqué unit on a background square. Align the needle in its right-hand position so that it virtually rubs the fold while stitching. Do not let the straight part of the stitch catch any part of the appliqué.

When the needle swings to the left, the appliqué will be caught. Keep your eye on the needle at all times as it makes the stitches straight. Go slowly so that you have control.

Practice corners and points to learn to make sure stitches secure both the sides and the actual point of points and corners. Points and corners are treated the same as with Blanket stitching. Review pages 64 if you are unfamiliar with these.

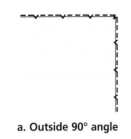

a. Outside 90° angle

b. Inside 90° angle

c. Inside 45° angle

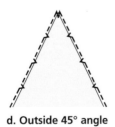

d. Outside 45° angle

To lock off the stitches, come back around to the beginning and stitch over the beginning stitches for ¹/₄".

These stitches are so tight and small that they are very unlikely to pull out. In fact, you will not want to have to take any of them out if you make a mistake. Sometimes it is easier to start over!

When working on multiple layers of the design, stitch the layers together before placing the pieces on the background fabric. An example of this is one heart on top of another: Stitch the small heart onto the larger heart first, then apply to the background fabric. This makes the job of removing the freezer paper much easier. If all the layers are sewn on top of each other through to the base fabric, you will later have to dig paper out of the very small channels, which is tedious and sometimes unsuccessful. Also, the appliqué will have a flat, stiff look.

Once you have your machine set to produce exactly the stitch you want, make note of the machine settings in your manual or sample notebook. Also make note of the top and bobbin tension settings. Now you have no excuses not to produce all those wonderful appliqué projects you just know you would never get done by hand!

Putting Theory into Practice

Now that you have read through pages and pages of instruction, put it to use by practicing with the Love Tulip pattern on page 93. Follow the directions step by step and you will end up with a lovely 12" appliqué square. You will use the freezer paper template method, which involves gluing the edges to the backside.

1. Begin by identifying the units of the pattern. There are two different hearts, two leaves, a stem, two different petals, and a bud. You will need a freezer paper pattern for every piece. Trace the units individually from the pattern onto freezer paper.

 For a further shortcut, refer to page 122 for information on using a photocopy machine to produce freezer paper templates.

2. Once the tracing is finished, cut out the freezer paper patterns as carefully as you can. On the wrong side of the fabrics, iron the freezer paper down securely. Leave 1/2" between all the template pieces.

3. Cut out the fabric, leaving a 3/16" seam allowance around all the edges.

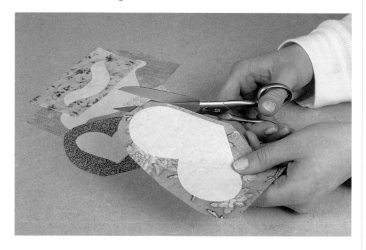

4. Next, examine the shapes to see where you will need to clip:

❋ At the cleavage of the hearts, make one clip straight down toward the paper, stopping one or two threads short of the paper.

❋ The shallow inside curve of the leaves and petals will need to be clipped with tiny bias clips that go halfway to the paper.

For more information on clipping see page 115.

5. Identify the edges that will not get turned under with "X"s. In this pattern, there are six of these edges. They are:

❋ the ends of the two leaves
❋ the bottom edge of the bud
❋ the bottom edge of the small petal
❋ the two ends of the stem

The photo also shows the inside curves that need to be clipped. You do not need to mark these on your units.

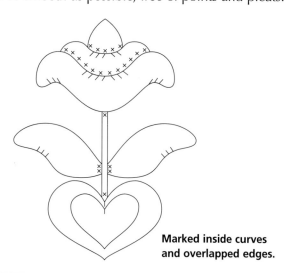

6. Turn all the remaining edges under, using the techniques discussed on page 115. Be very careful to keep the edges as smooth as possible, free of points and pleats.

Marked inside curves and overlapped edges.

Tip *When turning the edge over the tips of the leaves and large petal, trim the seam allowance to 1/8" if necessary. Using very tiny pinches with the tips of your fingers, twist slightly as you turn the seam allowance over and pinch. This will ease in the fullness. On curves like this, it is often helpful to start in the center and work out in each direction to ease in fullness.*

7. Before placing the shapes on the background fabric, align the small heart on top of the large heart and appliqué in place. Repeat with the three flower units. Refer to page 81 for instructions on gluing units together before stitching.

Tip *When stitching into the inside points as at the top of the heart, manually control the machine feed so that you can make sure there are adequate bites of the zigzag stitch to hold down the point. This can also be achieved by shortening the stitch length. Once out of this area, return to the longer stitch length.*

Now, pin all the shapes in place onto a 12½" square of background fabric. Position the tulip either diagonally or straight. Simply lay the background fabric on top of the pattern, aligning the crease lines with the pattern for centering, and position the shapes. Secure them with very fine pins or glue baste it (see page 83).

This pattern can be stitched almost continuously. You will need to start and stop only three times total to jump over the stem. Follow with the instructions below and the illustration on page 93.

1. Start at the lower edge of the left leaf. Backstitch a couple of tiny stitches in the beginning. Stitch around the entire leaf (1-4).

2. When you get to the stem, backstitch, drag the thread over the stem (do not cut the thread) and position the needle at the top of the right leaf, backstitch. Stitch around the right leaf (5-7), and once you get to the stem again, pivot down the stem toward the heart (8).

3. Pivot again to go around the large heart (9-14). (The small heart should have been stitched earlier before laying out the units onto the background fabric). Once you get to the stem, keep going (15) in order to stitch the inside point of the large heart. You will stop on the right side of the stem. Backstitch.

4. Now drag the thread back across the stem, so that the needle is positioned on the left side of the stem, heading toward the flower. Stitch up to the flower (16), then pivot (17) and stitch around the perimeter of the flower (18–24).

5. The individual units should have been stitched together before laying out the units onto the background fabric. Once you arrive back to the stem, again keep going (25) until you are at the left side of the stem. Backstitch.

6. Drag the thread to the right side of the stem and backstitch. Stitch down the stem (26) to the bottom of the right leaf and backstitch. You are finished!

When stitching, take your time and concentrate on the needle being as close to the edge of the appliqué as possible without stitching on top of the edge. This way, the stitching will be invisible and the swing stitch will just barely show. Pivot as necessary to control the curve. To pivot, stop with the needle in the fabric when in the right position, and move the fabric slightly to realign the edge with the needle. Do this as many times as necessary to keep the needle in proper alignment. Refer to page 65 for more information on pivoting around curves.

As you come to the tips of the large petal, slow down and carefully pivot around the curve. Make sure that several swing stitches are catching the appliqué so that the tiny seam allowance won't have a chance of fraying out. These are fragile areas and usually the first to fray, so pay special attention to them. When you stitch the large heart, make sure that you anchor the inside point at the top of the heart.

When all the stitching is completed, turn the block over and carefully cut the background fabric away, cutting 1/4" inside the stitching lines. When you have removed the base fabric of the large heart, gently tear the freezer paper from inside the stitching of the small heart. Now cut 1/4" inside this stitching line (you will be cutting the large heart fabric this time). This exposes the paper inside the smaller heart.

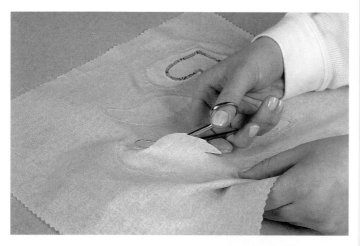

After cutting the backing, either submerge the whole block in warm water, or use a spray bottle and wet the seam allowance areas—anywhere the glue stick was used. Water will dissolve the glue. Gently peel the paper out of the appliqué pieces. The freezer paper should roll out easily if it is wet enough.

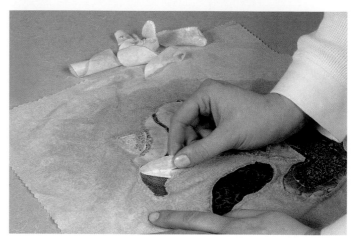

Blot the block dry, and press from the backside of the block. Use a permanent press setting on your iron.

Tip *It is very important that you do NOT use a hot iron when pressing appliqué using nylon thread, as you can melt the thread with the hot iron. Use a perma-press or synthetic setting when pressing.*

Congratulations! When you turn the block over, you will be delighted at how beautiful the stitching is. It looks just like, and sometimes better than, hand stitching. You will also be pleased with the durability of this technique. Now appliqué quilts are as easy as strip piecing! Try Hawaiian Quilting with this method; the results are beautiful.

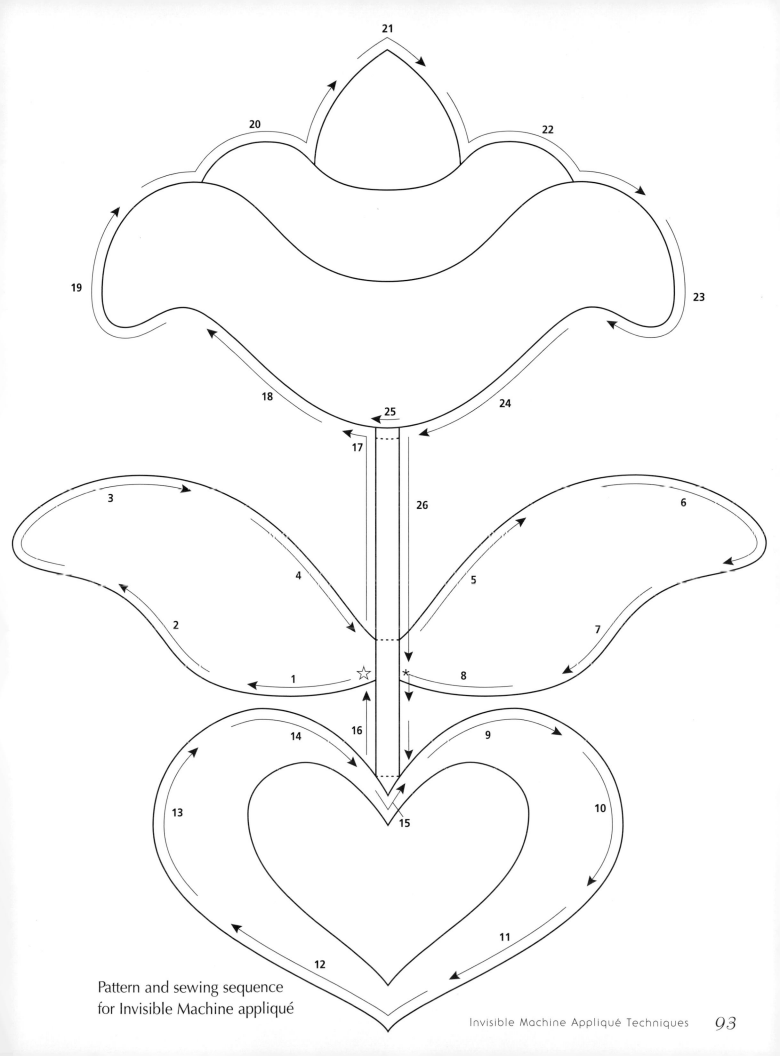

Pattern and sewing sequence
for Invisible Machine appliqué

Curved Piecing à la Appliqué

How many of you just can't wait to start a curved piecing project? Few machine piecers enjoy the process of cutting out each unit with a template, clipping and pinning the two curved edges, lining them up under the foot, and trying to sew accurately enough that the curve turns out to be a curve! Besides this, the size of the block is limited to 2" or larger to even be able to work with it under the presser foot. What if we could make curved piecing easier than sewing a straight line?

Drunkard's Path

This favorite block is a snap to make with my curved piece technique. Another method that is very similar is called the curved two-patch system. Joyce Scholtzhauer popularized this technique in the 1980s with her books *The Curved Two Patch System, Curves Unlimited,* and *Cutting Up with Curves.* Even though these books are out of print, they are excellent resources for design and inspiration, and the grid can be any size you want. Check your local public and quilt guild libraries for copies.

1. Begin by making two templates, one for the background square and one for the curved piece that will be applied to the background. Draw two 4" squares on graph paper. Add 1/4" seam allowance to one square, and glue the graph paper to cardboard, plastic, etc., to make a template. Example: If your finished block is a 4" square, cut this template 4 1/2" square. Do not cut the concave (inside) curve from this square. This will be the background square onto which the pie-shaped template unit is appliquéd. Cut the number of fabric squares needed (total number of blocks) for your project.

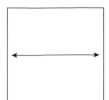

Square without seam allowances

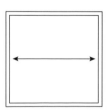

Square with seam allowances

94   Mastering Machine Appliqué

2. On the second square, make two marks that are approximately three-quarters of the length of any two adjacent sides.

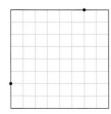

3/4 the length of 2 adjacent sides

3. Position the point of a compass at the corner. Place the pencil end of the compass on the mark on one side of the square. Draw an arc to the mark on the adjacent side.

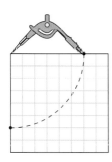

4. Draw in ¼" seam allowances for the right-angle corner, but do not add a seam allowance to the curve. Make a template for this piece.

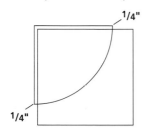

5. Trace the new pie-shaped template onto freezer paper, making one freezer paper pattern for every block needed. To speed this process, use the photo-copier method discussed on page 122, or use Harriet's Curved Piecing à la Appliqué templates. You could also try cutting multiple layers of paper if you have good cutting skills.

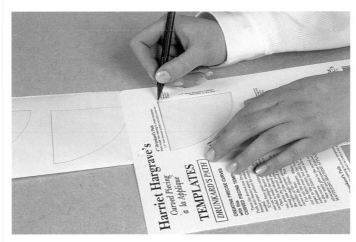

6. Cut out the freezer paper patterns, being careful to make the curved edge smooth.

7. Once the pie-shaped paper units are cut, press the freezer paper onto the wrong side of the desired fabrics. Keep the right-angle corner straight with the grainline of the fabric. This will put the curve on the bias.

Tip *Cut strips the needed width, then cut them into squares to be used with the templates. The squares will allow you to place the template exactly in the corner, aligning both sides perfectly. This is faster and more accurate than cutting all three sides around the paper template.*

8. Cut out the shapes. When cutting, cut the fabric even with the freezer paper in the corner if it wasn't pressed onto a square. Add a $3/16''$ extension of fabric to the curve for seam allowance.

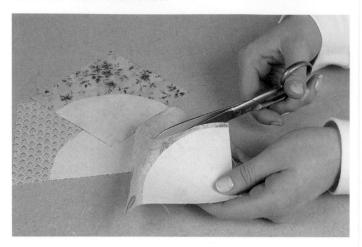

9. Using a fresh fabric-basting glue stick, apply glue to the curved seam allowance. Also apply a small amount of glue onto the edge of the freezer paper. Carefully roll the seam allowance over to the freezer paper with small pinch-and-twist motions of your thumb and fingertip. (See page 115 for detailed instructions on gluing.) This is the trick: You can get a more precise curve from gluing than from stitching the seam!

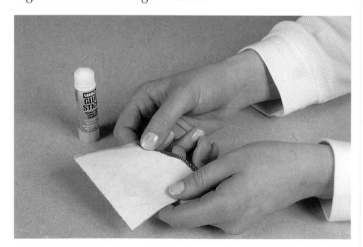

10. After all the curved edges are glued, you are ready to appliqué them to the squares discussed in Step One. Position the pie-shaped piece on top of the square so that the corners align exactly. Pin into place.

Tip *You will find that with experience, you will be able to hold the units together without pinning. The units will pivot through the machine by placing a finger as a pressure point to the left of the foot while sewing.*

11. With the machine set to do Invisible Machine appliqué and using invisible thread (see page 84), stitch the curve onto the square. Be careful that the needle rubs the curve when stitching straight. You do not want to be able to see any of the stitching. These units can be chain-sewn to save time and thread.

12. After all the curves are stitched into place, turn the square over. Cut away the corner of the square, leaving a ³/₁₆" seam allowance beyond the stitching. (Keep these pieces; they are perfect for another project, in a smaller grid. The corner is already square. Just apply a smaller pie-shaped piece of freezer paper and repeat the process above.)

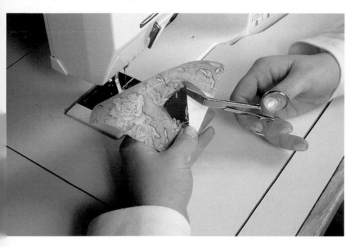

If using a basting glue stick, dampen the curved seam allowance that was glued to dissolve the glue. Gently pull the freezer paper out of this seam, and press from the wrong side. Assemble the blocks into any design or pattern you choose. This is an extremely accurate method. Because all of the pie-shaped pieces are identical and positioned the same way, the distance from the curved seam end to the corners is always the same. This is not always the case when piecing a curved seam.

Clamshells

The Clamshell pattern can be done using the same method as Drunkard's Path. This pattern used to be considered appropriate only for quilters with a great deal of experience, time, and patience. Now beginners will have perfect results, instantly!

Instead of viewing this as a patchwork pattern, let's turn it into an appliqué. Invisible Machine appliqué will make the block more accurate as well as stronger when finished.

1. Use the pattern for the clamshell shape on page 99, or draft your own. To do this, simply choose the size clamshell you want and draw a circle, with that diameter, using a compass. Draw a line through the center of the circle, making sure that the line intersects with the hole from the compass.

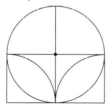

2. With a T-square or C-Thru® ruler, draw a line perpendicular to the first line intersecting the center hole.

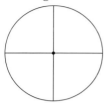

3. Draw lines that extend parallel to both of the center lines to create squares at the bottom corners of the circle.

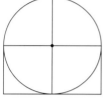

4. Place the point of the compass in these corners, one at a time, and draw in a curve that will cut the original circle at the half and bottom quarter points.

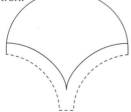

5. Before cutting out the shape, add ¹/₄" seam allowances to the new curved lines. Do not add seam allowance to the outer curve at the top. This is your template. You can either use the template method with spray starch (see page 77 for instructions) or make individual freezer paper patterns, using a fabric-basting glue stick.

6. If using freezer paper patterns, you are now ready to trace this shape as many times as needed onto freezer paper (or use the copy machine). Cut out the freezer paper shapes, keeping the outer curve as accurate as possible. Press these paper pieces onto the wrong side of the desired fabric. Cut the shapes out of the fabric, cutting even with the freezer paper on the inside curves at the bottom, but cutting a 3/16" extension of seam allowance on the upper, outside curve.

7. Using a glue stick, glue the outside curves over the freezer paper, keeping them smooth. Do not clip these curves.

8. After the raw edges have been glued over the paper, the shells are ready to be placed on the base fabric. Prepare your base fabric as follows: Placement begins from the top and works to the bottom. Lay the first horizontal row of shells in a straight line across the top of the base fabric. Stitch in place, using the Invisible Machine appliqué or Blanket stitch, whichever look you prefer. Stitch only around the large outside curve.

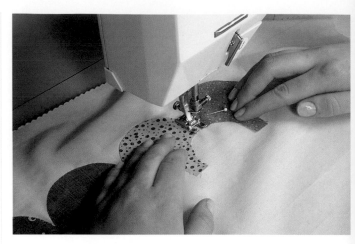

9. After the first row is stitched in place, remove the freezer paper, if it was used.

10. Position the second row of shells, making sure that the top curve lines up with and covers the seam allowances of the first row. Pin in place and stitch as for the first row. Continue these steps until all the rows have been sewn in place and all the paper has been removed.

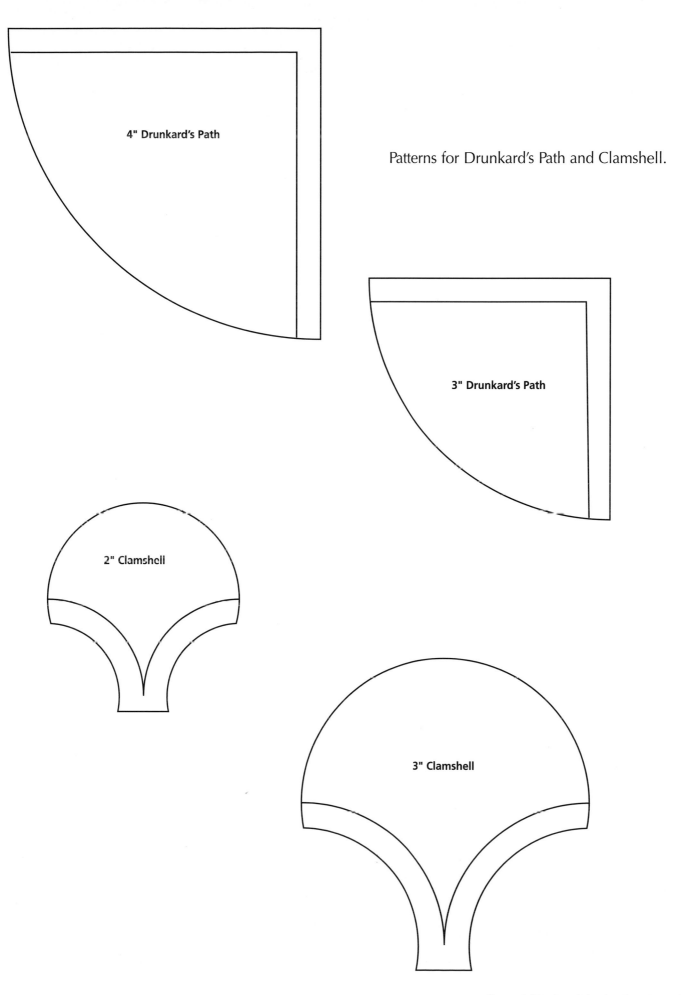

4" Drunkard's Path

Patterns for Drunkard's Path and Clamshell.

3" Drunkard's Path

2" Clamshell

3" Clamshell

Straight Stitch Appliqué

Straight stitch appliqué has been used on quilts to achieve beautiful, durable appliqué since the early 1860s. This method provides a very sturdy edge with visible stitching, but it does not have the heavy, bulky feel of Satin stitch appliqué. The technique involves folding the edge over, as with Invisible Machine appliqué.

Some pattern adaptations are helpful in preparing the pieces for stitching. It will be easier to prepare the edges if you slightly round any sharp inside corners and create gentle curves. See the illustration below.

Round off sharp curves

Round off deep curves

NOTE: Any of the preparation methods that are used for Invisible Machine appliqué (Chapter Twelve) can be used for this technique. Your choice will be determined by whether you want to cut the backs out and how detailed the pattern pieces are. After experimenting with the various options, you will know which one suits the pattern you are working with.

The following brief instructions are for working with the template and spray starch method. The Love Tulip pattern given on page 58 or any pattern of your choice can be used to work through this technique.

Trace pattern pieces onto Templar, making a pattern for every unit of the design. The line that is drawn and cut from the template material will represent the finished edge of the appliqué itself, so accuracy is extremely important. Make note of the pieces that need to be cut in reverse if your pattern is not symmetrical.

Following the guidelines for grainline on page 71, place the templates on the wrong side of the fabric. Leave at least $1/2$" between each template. Trace around each shape, repeating as often as needed for the design.

Carefully cut $3/16$" to $1/4$" seam allowances around the outside of the traced line. Clip inside points and curves, and identify edges that will be under another piece and not turned over.

♥ NOTE: **The width you cut the seam allowance is determined by your ability to work with the point of the iron over a template edge. The narrower the seam allowance, the nicer the edge, but the more difficult it is to work with when using an iron. Experiment until you can get the edge you want. This is where the Clover Mini Iron is very helpful.**

Lay the pieces on the ironing board wrong side up, and position the template within the traced lines. Using your fingertip or a paintbrush, apply spray starch to the seam allowances and press over the edge of the template. Press until dry.

Tip *Press sharp points first, then concave (inside) areas, then straighter areas. Continue this until all seam allowances—except edges that are extensions—are pressed over. Carefully remove the templates and press again from the front side of the appliqué. The edges should be smooth and crisp.*

If you have trouble getting circles and near circular shapes smooth and even, try this: Using thread that matches your fabric, carefully sew (by machine or hand) a line of gathering stitches in the seam allowance. This will help distribute the extra fullness in the seam allowance when it is turned over. Place the template on the shape, and pull up the gathering thread. Evenly distribute the fullness and press.
Carefully remove the template.

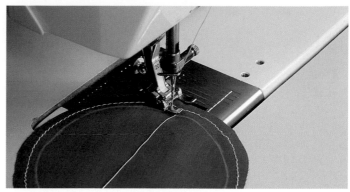
Gathering stitch in seam allowance

Pulling up gathering thread around template

Prepare background fabric by folding in half lengthwise, crosswise, then diagonally, and pressing lightly to place registration lines, see page 82. Center this block over the pattern and begin placing the pattern pieces where they belong. Pin securely, or use spots of glue stick to hold in place.

Prepare your sewing machine by threading the top and bobbin with matching 50/2 or 60/2-embroidery thread. 30/2 thread can be used for top thread if a heavier stitch is desired. Invisible nylon can also be used for top thread if you like its appearance. Experiment. Use the needle size appropriate for the thread you choose. Refer to Chapter One, page 12, for a helpful chart.

You have a choice of machine feet to work with for this method. You can either use the open-toe appliqué foot that we have been using up to now, or you can change to an edge-stitching foot, if one is available for your machine. This foot resembles the blind-stitch foot, but does not have the easement bar across the center.

The guiding bar is kept next to the edge of the appliqué, and the needle position is adjusted to where you want the stitch on the appliqué edge.

The stitch is sewn approximately 1/16" from the folded edge of the appliqué piece. Adjust the needle position of the machine to the distance you prefer. Use your straight stitch throat plate instead of the normal zigzag plate; your machine makes a nicer straight stitch and gives you accuracy in pivoting and easing. Set the stitch length for 12 stitches per inch, or between 2 and 2 1/2. Sew a sample to check tension settings and stitch length before stitching the appliqué.

Starting with the pieces on the bottom layer, stitch along the edge of the appliqué. Go slowly around curves and points, keeping the stitch distance from the edge as exact and even as you can. Pivot when necessary. Change color of thread when fabric color changes. To lock off your stitches when changing thread colors, lift the appliqué piece that is on top of the piece you are currently stitching, and begin stitching with the new color thread at the top piece's raw edge.

Lift top piece to lock off threads

Continue around and end at the top piece's raw edge. Repeat this for each additional layer. When the next layer is stitched, it will catch and hold the thread tails of the lower piece. On the very top piece, do either a short backstitch, make several tiny short stitches, or take the threads to the back and secure by tying and adding a small drop of Fray Check®.

CHAPTER 18

Broderie Perse

Broderie Perse is the technique of appliquéing chintz fabrics onto a background fabric. These chintz prints are cut out and arranged into a design on the base fabric. The appliqué can be made from one cut piece or from several cut pieces, which are rearranged and overlapped to create a collage effect.

The French words *broderie perse* mean "Persian embroidery." This technique was popular in America during the eighteenth century for bedcoverings. Traditionally, the cutouts were pasted onto a background fabric that was stretched in a frame. Once the paste was dry, the fabric was taken out of the frame, and the cutouts were stitched down with invisible stitches. You will be adapting these techniques for machine stitching.

Photographs of antique chintz quilts, Baltimore Album quilts, and floral appliqué quilts are good sources of inspiration for the design process. Most of the fabrics are printed in a repeat pattern, and the mirror image of the design is not available. This requires you to cut the design apart so that you can rotate, cut off, and rearrange individual parts to get the design to face opposite directions and give you the finished design you desire.

The following ideas are only that—ideas. Experiment and see how you can adapt other traditional hand appliqué techniques, such as Hawaiian quilting, to your sewing machine.

Blanket Stitching (Raw Edge)

If you choose to use a Blanket stitch to appliqué the chintz pieces onto the background fabric, you will be working with a raw edge that has a fusing agent applied to it to keep the edges from fraying.

1. Working with fabric that has large printed flowers on it, select and cut out your desired flowers. Leave about an inch of fabric around each selected shape.

Selecting flowers for appliqué

2. Photocopy the backside (fabric will be right side up) of each of these pieces. If the units are larger than a sheet of paper, you will need to divide the large piece into quadrants so you will be able to reassemble the photocopied pieces to the original shape. This produces a mirror image of the print.

Photocopy fabric

♥ **HINT: If you have a high-powered lightbox, you might be able trace directly from the fabric. Turn the fabric right side down on the light box and lay the fusible, paper side up, directly on top of the fabric. Trace.**

3. Using a dark-colored pen and, if available, a light-box, trace around the outside of the photocopied flower so you will have a guide to use when tracing the shape onto the paper-backed fusible web.

Trace around flowers

4. Place fusible web, paper side up, over the outlined photocopy of your fabric and trace the outline you just marked onto the paper-backed fusible web.

Trace onto fusible web

5. Once all your patterns are traced onto the fusible web, cut out the center of each of these pieces, leaving about 1/4" of web inside the traced line and an inch outside the traced line to match the fabric (refer to Chapter Five, pages 40-41).

Cutting inside the traced line

6. Match your cut fusible pieces with the backside of your fabric units, lining up the traced lines. Press following manufacturer's instructions.

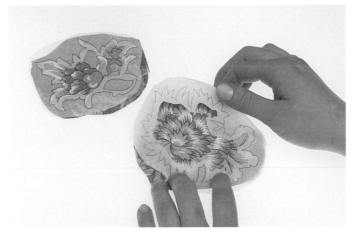

Matching fusible pieces with fabric pieces

7. Cut out the flower, cutting from the right side of the fabric for accuracy.

Cutting out flowers from the right side of the fabric

8. If stems are extremely narrow, leave a margin of about 1/8" of fabric to make stitching easier.

9. Remove the paper backing from the fusible web.

10. Arrange onto background fabric and fuse in place

11. Do a small Buttonhole stitch around every raw edge. You may want to add Satin stitching on the design lines of internal flowers for effect.

When stitching the edges, consider changing the top thread color to match the fabric as it changes color. This has a beautiful blending effect, and the stitches become part of the fabric, instead of an outline or frame around the print. However, there might be a time when a contrasting thread would highlight a certain print. The quilt shown on page 132 is an example. Because the flowers farthest out into the background are so light, I decided to stitch them with a brown thread to outline them. This worked well with the print, as there was a brown outline around most of the design to start with.

Invisible Machine Appliqué

If you want an invisible stitch around the Broderie Perse design, use the Invisible Machine appliqué technique. Making the freezer paper patterns will be the tricky part, and before beginning, read Chapter Twenty for tips about using a photocopy machine. I find it an invaluable tool for Broderie Perse appliqué.

Method #1—Photocopied Patterns

1. Place the chintz design, fabric right side up, on the photocopy machine and copy. This will produce a mirror image of the fabric.

2. Lay a sheet of freezer paper, plastic side down, on top of the photocopy pattern. Carefully trace in the details that you want along the folded edge. This process will give you a pattern that duplicates the print edge of the chintz, instead of leaving a margin of background fabric that will show later.

3. Cut out the tracing along the line.

4. Position the freezer paper pattern on the wrong side of the chintz, aligning the edge of the paper to the print line of the design. Press.

5. Cut out each chintz design, leaving a ³/₁₆" seam allowance along all edges. Clip and trim as necessary (refer to page 115 if you need information).

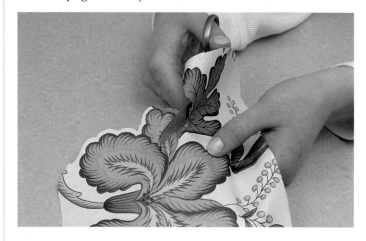

6. Roll the fabric edges over the edge of the freezer paper and glue them in place with a fresh glue stick. Check to be sure that the finished edge is along the print line of the fabric.

7. Design and position the cutouts onto the base fabric.

8. Stitch, following the instructions in Chapter Fifteen. Cut away the parts of the background fabric underneath the chintz to remove the paper. This will also eliminate the bulk and make the quilting softer.

Method #2—Photocopying onto Freezer Paper

Having a photocopy machine available will save hours of tracing time. This method is basically the same as Method #1, except that the pattern is photocopied directly onto the freezer paper. This method is limited to chintz pieces the size of a sheet of paper, unless you want to work with pieces by overlapping and butting them.

Photocopy fabric onto freezer paper

1. Cut freezer paper into sheets the same size as the copier paper. Feed in each sheet manually, with the freezer paper plastic side down on top of a sheet of copier paper. This protects the freezer paper from the heat of the machine, see page 122.

2. Place the chintz cutout right side up on the copier.

3. Manually feed the freezer paper/copier paper sandwich into the machine. The fabric design will be copied directly onto the freezer paper, eliminating the need to trace the copy onto the freezer paper.

4. Carefully cut the copy out on the print line and press onto wrong side of chintz, aligning edges exactly.

5. Continue with steps 5 through 8 of Method #1.

For detailed information about Broderie Perse and other techniques used to create chintz quilts, look for a copy of *Chintz Quilts: Unfading Glory* by Shiell and Bullard. I hope the book, along with the many beautiful decorator fabrics available, will inspire you to create one of these beauties.

CHAPTER 19

Stained Glass

Stained Glass appliqué has come and gone and come again in popularity with quilters. While never totally out of fashion, its popularity has been inconsistent unlike that of appliqué and pieced quilts.

The Blind stitch on your sewing machine makes creating a Stained Glass piece very easy. If you have never tried this form of appliqué, do so now. Today's vibrantly colored fabrics—cottons, lamés, satins, silks, etc.—produce truly luminescent "windows" of cloth.

Designs

You will find designs and patterns for Stained Glass appliqué from many sources; not surprisingly, the most appropriate designs come from patterns for actual stained glass. These can be purchased from a stained glass store and be reduced or enlarged to make a master pattern.

Copy or trace the original design onto paper to make a master pattern. Trace the individual pieces onto the paper side of freezer paper. Do not add seam allowance. The pieces will be cut on the design line and the raw edges butted snugly to one another, just like a jigsaw puzzle. You do not need to do reverse image tracings because the paper will be applied to the right side of the fabric. Number the pieces so you can identify them when you are ready to lay out the design. Carefully cut the units apart. Leave the master pattern intact; it will be used for the layout.

Pattern traced and cut apart

Fabrics

The fabrics will be easier to work with if they are backed with an iron-on interfacing or a fusible web. If the finished piece is to be used as a bed quilt instead of a wall hanging, use a very soft interfacing, or spray-starch the fabrics three times to give the fabric extra body. Choose the method you want to use on your fabrics and prepare them in this manner.

Press the freezer paper pattern units onto the right side of the fabrics. Carefully cut along the line traced on the paper. Cut each piece accurately so that the pieces of the design fit back together tightly.

Press freezer paper onto fabric

After cutting out the units, prepare the background fabric by folding it into fourths and pressing in registration lines. Lay the fabric on top of the original pattern and center. If your pattern is in sections, you may want to make a full-scale layout of the finished design to use for placement. Mark the centering registration lines on the pattern to be used to line up with the background fabric. Pin the two together.

Preparing background fabric

 If your base fabric is dark or if you have problems seeing through it, the use of a lightbox or other light source is indispensable.

Bias Strips for Lead Lines

You can either use purchased bias tape or make your own. Making your own bias gives you more flexibility in color and fabric selection and is not that time consuming. Purchased tape is easier, but color selection and quality might be inadequate. There are now rolls of pre-folded fusible bias available.

The lead lines for Stained Glass appliqué should be $1/4"$ or smaller. Be sure that the strips are true bias, because tight curves require the stretching ability of bias. Refer to page 117, for making perfect bias for this technique.

After all the appliqué pieces are prepared, you are ready to build the design onto the background fabric. It is very helpful to use a light box for this process. The light box allows you to place the fabric on top of the pattern and see through the fabric for placement.

Assembly

Examine the original pattern to see if there are any "lead lines" placed in the background, such as squares or diagonals to create a grid effect behind the colored "glass." If there are, these pieces of bias must be placed and stitched first, for an example see page 133.

Position the pattern units on the background fabric, aligning the edges for a tight fit.

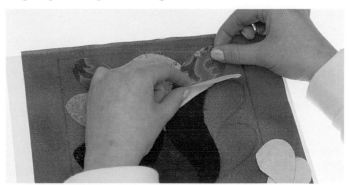

Position units on background

Once the "glass" pieces are placed and secured, you can begin to place the bias. If you are not working with fusible bias, attach the bias with pins, glue stick, or basting.

Before applying the bias to the piece, examine where short pieces will be used and where long pieces will run continuously. The short pieces should be applied first and fused or stitched in place. Their raw ends will then be covered by the longer pieces. Take the time to ease accurately around difficult curves and points.

Place short bias strips

All bias in place

Tip *Bias can be formed into curves and shapes at the ironing board with a steam iron. Lay the bias in the shape desired, and set the shape with steam. The bias will assume and keep this shape as you position it onto the project.*

Stitching

Set your machine to do a small zigzag stitch. Use 60 weight/2-ply black (or matching color) machine embroidery thread in the top and bobbin of the machine. Smoke colored invisible nylon thread can also be used with 60/2 black in the bobbin. Put the open-toe appliqué foot or the edge-stitch foot on the machine. Use a size 70 needle. Stitch both sides of the tape, letting the swing of the needle go just off the edge of the tape onto the "glass" fabric. This tiny stitch gives a hand-stitched appearance to your work. See Chapter 15 to review Invisible Machine appliqué techniques as needed.

Tip *To prevent distortion, work with a pin or stiletto in your hand to help ease the tape under the foot. After all the bias is stitched into place, finish the piece by quilting, bordering, binding, or framing.*

Double Needle Stitching

With a little practice, you might find this technique fast and easy—in a single operation you can stitch both edges of the bias. This method of stitching is particularly applicable to straight lines and gentle curves. If your pattern has a lot of tight curves, you may want to rethink stitching with a double needle. At the least, make some practice pieces before starting the project.

Double needles come in several different spacing choices between the needles. For $1/4$" bias be sure that you purchase a 4mm double needle so that the two needles each stitch along an edge of the bias. Refer to your sewing machine manual as to how to correctly thread your machine to use two threads at once.

When stitching, sew slowly so that you have total control of both needles. On tighter curves, use the hand wheel to slowly walk the needles through the curve. Lift the needles out of the fabric until they are just barely touching the bias. Lift the presser foot and pivot the fabric slightly. Lower the presser foot and hand-guide the needles into the bias.

Using a double needle

To lock off stitches, either backstitch one or two stitches at the beginning and end of each section, or take the top threads to the back and tie them with the bobbin thread, applying a drop of Fray Check to the knot.

Reverse Appliqué Stained Glass
by Cathy Robiscoe

Cathy Robiscoe, a quilter from Bozeman, Montana, developed an extraordinary new technique for Stained Glass appliqué using reverse appliqué techniques and freezer paper. Cathy shared this method with shop owners at the October 1991 International Quilt Market. Below is a brief explanation of her technique. Cathy has designed a line of Stained Glass patterns which include very detailed instructions for her technique.

If using one of Cathy's patterns, you will find that the lead lines are all $1/4"$ wide, instead of the standard single line. If you are using a standard stained glass pattern, use a double pencil, (tape two pencils together), to trace over the lines to create the $1/4"$ lead line. Keep the single original line in the center, between the new lines being traced.

1. Use a piece of freezer paper larger than the pattern. Glue the edges of two pieces together, if necessary to cover a larger pattern. The paper needs to be in one piece.

2. Trace the stained glass pattern onto the freezer paper. Check to see if reverse image drawing is necessary. Trace each of the double lines $1/4"$ apart. These will be the "lead" of the finished piece.

3. Lay the freezer paper on your rotary cutter mat, and with a single-blade art knife, carefully cut along each line. You will be cutting out the area where the colored "glass" will be showing. The remaining paper forms "lead" lines.

4. After all the units are cut and removed, carefully lay the freezer paper pattern onto a piece of solid black fabric (or color of your choice), and press to secure the freezer paper to the fabric.

5. Working with only a few sections at a time in a small area, carefully cut the black fabric 3/16" from the freezer paper. Clip any inside curves halfway to the paper, and clip any corners up to one thread from the paper.

6. Using a glue stick, apply glue to the seam allowance and the freezer paper. Let dry, then gently roll the seam allowance over onto the paper. Work on a flat surface when doing this to prevent distorting the pattern. Cathy recommends using a round toothpick to help manipulate the seam allowance.

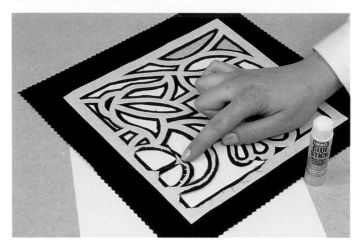

7. Once you have a few sections prepared, carefully turn the black over, and place the desired color under one of the openings. Dabbing a few spots of glue on the paper back will help secure the colored "glass" in place while stitching.

8. Using a small zigzag stitch, stitch around the opening with 60/2 black machine-embroidery thread. Position the needle to just rub the black folded edge, but stitch in the "glass" when the needle is in the right swing. This will give a hand-stitched appearance.

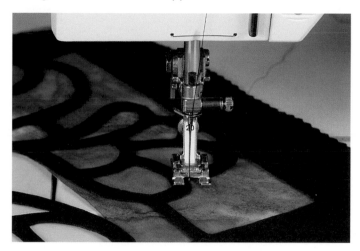

When stitching, carefully pivot around curves and secure points as discussed in Chapter Fifteen.

9. Once the area is stitched, turn the piece over and carefully trim the excess fabric 1/8" – 3/16" from the stitching.

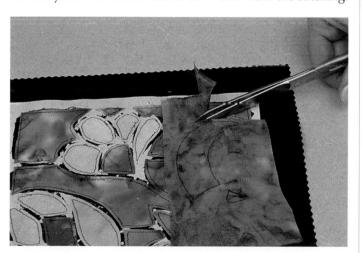

Step 9

10. Continue adding the colored "glass" in the same manner. The finished product is neat, accurate and beautiful.

Reverse appliqué techniques can be adapted to many uses other than Stained Glass. Let your imagination and creativity carry you away.

Keep Creating!

I hope by now you are dreaming up lots of ideas for using machine appliqué. Now, instead of just admiring others' work, you will, as many of my students do, get "instant gratification" from creating your own.

CHAPTER 20

Tips, Tricks, and Other Useful Information

I've learned many tricks and tips about appliqué and other quilt making techniques over the years and would like to share them here with you.

Cutting

Accuracy in cutting freezer paper or any other template material is most critical. The condition of the cut edge of your template will directly affect the finished edge of the appliqué. I can't stress enough how important it is to take great care when cutting your templates.

Rough edges on the freezer paper templates or the tagboard templates will produce appliqué shapes with the same rough edges. Cut precisely and use very sharp scissors for both paper and fabric. If you have difficulty with cutting, try keeping the scissors steady and move the fabric or paper through them. By turning the fabric or paper instead of the scissors, the blades keep a consistent tension, allowing you to make smoother cuts.

The standard seam allowance used in appliqué is $3/16$", which gives the best results when turning the edges over. If your seam allowance is $1/4$" or wider, the bulk creates small pleats in the fabric, which form points along the folded edge of the appliqué, forcing you to clip every edge to fit the bulk into the smaller space. If the seam allowance is less than $3/16$", it is so small that handling will cause raveling, and laundering will fray the few threads left. A $3/16$" width gives a perfect edge without excess clipping or fraying. (Learning to eyeball this measurement will speed the cutting time considerably. View it as a fat eighth or a skinny quarter.)

Different widths of seam allowances

Clipping

A basic guideline to prevent frayed edges is NEVER clip outside (convex) curves; only clip inside (concave) curves. If your seam allowances are too large, clipping is necessary, but too often the end result is pointed edges and frayed clips. The small seam allowance used here eliminates the need to clip outside curves. Inside curves, however, need to be clipped so that the fabric can expand to the larger area when turned under.

When clipping inside curves, clip the seam allowance only halfway to the edge of freezer paper. Examine the grainline of the seam allowance, and try to make your clip on the bias grain of the seam allowance in order to deter fraying. You will often need to make a diagonal rather than a perpendicular clip.

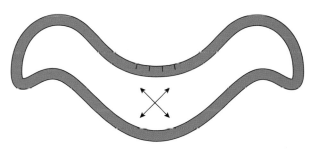

Clip with the bias grain

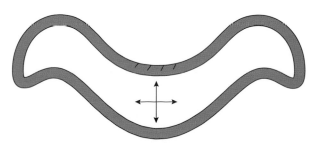

Clip with the bias grain

You will also need to clip inside points, as with hearts. One clip, straight down to within one thread of the paper, is all that is needed for inside points. Do not overclip!

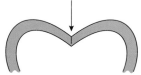

Carefully clip at inside point

Turning Smooth Edges

When rolling a $3/16$" seam allowance to the back side of an appliqué piece, use care and a light touch. Whether gluing or pressing the seam allowance into position, be careful to work with only small increments at a time, and treat the edge like delicate pastry.

Beginning along a straight or slightly curved edge, gently roll the seam allowance over the freezer paper or tagboard template edge, and pinch the glued edges together or press with the very tip of the iron. If gluing, use the tip of your thumb and work only the very edge of the paper. Do not take large "bites" with your thumb, but instead, take tiny little pinches. As you come to the curves, pinch and twist at the same time, again taking tiny bites with the tip of your thumb. (This will remind you of the pinch and twist motion used to make fluted pie crust.)

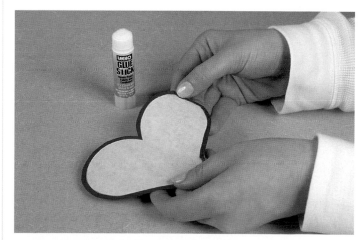

Gently roll seam allowance over paper edge

If using an iron, try to finger-press the edges to form them before using the iron. Keep your fingers as close as you dare to the iron to control the edge. Take your time with this process.

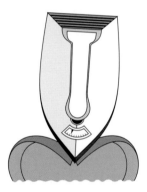

Turning edge with iron

Perfect Points

When turning the edges over in preparation for stitching, points can be the most difficult area to handle. There are different ways of handling points, depending on the degree of the angle. Try different techniques on samples to master these tricky areas.

Method #1

I find this the easiest way to obtain perfect points, but it does require you to make plenty of tiny stitches at the point to hold the fabric edge down completely when stitching.

1. Press or glue to the very end of the first side of the point or corner. Be sure to keep the seam allowance even and straight all the way to the end of the fabric.

2. Now fold the other side over, pressing or gluing it straight, taking it all the way off the end of the point.

3. Using very sharp small scissors, clip off the seam allowance fabric that extends beyond the point.

This gives a perfect point, even for very acute points, every time. When stitching, be sure that several tiny stitches catch the edge along both sides of the point, as well as the very point itself.

Method #2

1. Fold the pointed end of the seam allowance down onto the wrong side on the appliqué. If using freezer paper, be careful not to bend it over.

2. Press or glue the seam allowance over the point on the right-hand side of the piece.

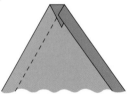

3. Press seam allowance over the point on the left-hand side of the piece. Trim seam allowance as needed.

Method #3

1. Press or glue the seam allowance to the very end of the first side of the point or corner.

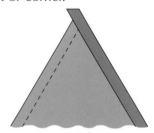

2. Press and glue the point over at a 45° angle, so that the point's seam allowance is over the left-side seam allowance. You might need to clip out some of the bulk of the point's seam allowance.

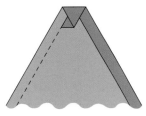

3. Press and glue the left seam allowance over. It is often helpful to use a pin or needle to fold the point over to keep it very pointed.

Tip *When working with small or slender shapes, it is helpful to trim the seam allowance to about 1/8" from paper's edge for ease in handling.*

Bias Strips For Stems

Many appliqué patterns call for tiny stems. These can be difficult to do, using any of the above techniques. Try following the bias methods of making stems of any size and choose the one that works best for you.

Find the true bias of the fabric by folding the corner over so that the crosswise grain lines up with the lengthwise grain (selvage). This will be true bias.

Bias strips are generally not wider than 1/2". For 1/2" finished bias strips, cut bias strips 1 1/4" wide. For 1/4" and narrower finished bias strips, cut strips 3/4" wide. Anything narrower than 3/4" cut is very difficult to handle.

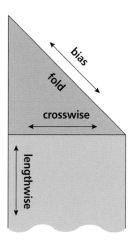

Tip *A very simple way to cut straight strips is to use a straight-edge ruler and a rotary cutter. If you find that the fabric moves too much, you can also use different widths of masking tape. Press the tape onto the bias of the fabric. Cut the strip along the edge of the masking tape. Carefully remove the tape after cutting. (Drafting tape is the easiest to remove.)*

1. After cutting the bias strip the desired width, fold the strip of bias in half lengthwise, wrong sides together.

2. Stitch the folded strip down its length along the raw edge. The raw edge is on your right, the fold on the left.

NOTE: The finished width of the stem is equal to the distance between this stitching and the folded edge.

3. Press, keeping the seam allowance in the center of the strip. Trim the raw edge, if necessary.

4. Stitch the folded edges down to the background fabric.

Method #2 — Bias Bars

Philomena Wiechek developed this method for her Celtic appliqué, and it is very successful.

1. Cut bias strip larger than the desired finished width and fold it in half lengthwise, wrong sides together.

2. Lay the bias bar on top of the folded strip, one edge against the fold. Draw a line along the opposite edge for the seamline.

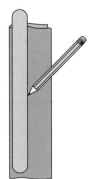

3. Stitch along the seamline. Trim excess seam allowance.

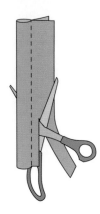

4. Slip the bias bar into the tube after stitching. Turn the tube so that the seam is centered down the length of the tube. Press the seam one direction. Trim seam allowance, if needed.

Method #3 – Bias or Straight Strips Through Pins

This method was shared by Nina Stalschmidt and Ang Whittaker of Canada. It works well for both bias and straight-grain strips to produce almost any size you need. Starch all fabrics heavily before cutting the strips. Place the pins in a square of heavy fabric. This will also protect the ironing board from scorching under the iron.

1. Cut strips using either bias or straight grain. The strip width is determined by multiplying the desired finished width by three. Cut generously, adding an extra $1/8"$ to the size. Cut long strips, as short strips are difficult to turn evenly. The strips will be cut to length needed at the time of layout. Leave them long for now.

Cut Size	Finished size
$5/8"$+	$3/16"$
$7/8"$	$1/4"$
$1 1/4"$	$3/8"$
$1 5/8"$	$1/2"$
$2"$	$5/8"$
$2 3/8"$	$3/4"$

2. At the end of each strip, start the folding process. Working with the right side out, fold the first inch of each strip into thirds lengthwise. Once the seam allowances are overlapped, the width of the folded strip should be the desired finished size. Crease the folds.

3. Fold a square of heavy fabric in half. Draw two parallel lines about 6" long and the width of the desired finished strip. Use any marking tool that leaves a very fine line. At one end of the line, take a stitch with a pin. The pin will come up at the first line, then go back into the fabric on the second line to complete the stitch. Once you have the pin at the first line, place the end of the folded strip under the pin, raw edges up. Take the pin across the strip and back into the fabric on the second line. The strip should fit tightly under the pin.

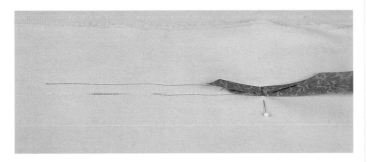

4. Using your thumb about 2" from the pin to help shape the strip, you will need to pull the strip under the pin and press as you go. It is advisable to use a hemostat (or tweezers) to hold onto the end to prevent burning your fingers. Place the point of the iron on the folded strip. Do this until you have pressed about 3" of fabric under the pin. Remove the iron.

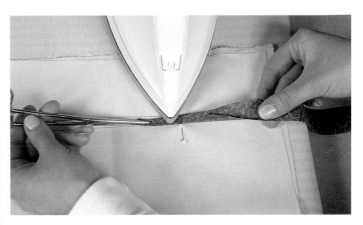

5. Place a second pin about 3" to 4" away from the first, pinning as you did the first time. Place the folded strip under the pin as you go.

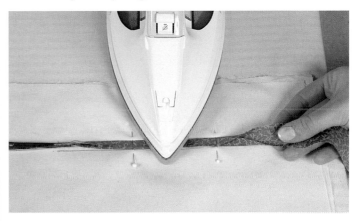

6. As you pull the strip through the pins, the strip will automatically fold. Hold the strip on both ends as you draw it through the pins. Place the tip of your iron between the pins, and press as you pull the strip through. The point of the iron will just sit on the strip; you do not need to hold it.

> *Tip* *Clover makes a wonderful tool known as the Bias Tape Maker. They come in a limited number of sizes (¼", ½" ¾", 1" and 2"), but are fast and easy if the available sizes fit your needs.*

Method #4—Using Bias for Tiny Stems

This method allows you to make stems as small as 1/8".
You will still need to work with a cut strip that is 3/4"
wide and trim the excess away once it is stitched in place.

1. Fold the bias strip in half lengthwise, wrong sides
together. Baste a line of stitching down the strip that is
the desired finished width from the fold.

2. Position and pin the basted strip onto the background. Lay the basted line along the outside curve if
there is one, raw edges to the inside of the curve.

3. Stitch just to the side of the basting, through the
background fabric.

4. Trim any excess seam allowance.

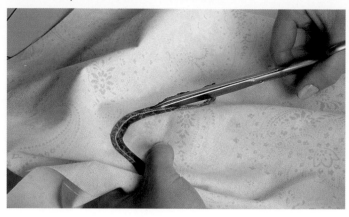

5. Roll the bias over the seam allowance and appliqué
the fold down.

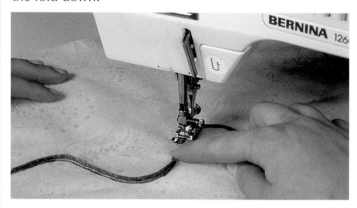

Tip *When sewing your strips or stems onto the background, it is often easier to stitch the inner curve
first. The bias will stretch along the outer curve when stitching
down. This is less difficult than easing in the fullness of the
inner curve after stretching the outer curve first.*

Method #5—Using Piping for Tiny Stems

This technique is another way to get tiny stems. If you have trouble keeping the stems for technique #4 even and straight, this technique might be the key for you. It is a form of mini-piping. The stems are made as corded piping. This technique will help you to make stems $1/16$" to $1/8$" wide. You will need a pintucking foot and cording of the size desired, such as #3 perle cotton.

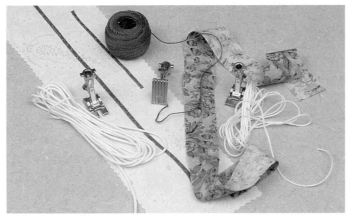

Piping materials

1. Begin by starching the fabric before cutting it into 1" wide bias strips. A general guideline for wider stems is to cut the fabric 1" wider than the finished width of the stem. Make the strips as long as possible. They will be cut to size later.

2 Fold the strip of fabric over the cording. Using the groove in the bottom of the piping foot will assist in guiding the cord and allow you to stitch as close to the cord as possible but not stitch into the cord. If you do not have a piping foot, a zipper foot will work.

> 🖊 *Tip* *Please refer to your machine manual on how to adjust your needle position to work with pintucking feet correctly. Pintuck feet have centered grooves, and if the needle is not in the correct position, it will sew down the center of the cord. You will need to position the needle so that it stitches directly beside the cord. Pintucking feet come with three, five, seven, and nine grooves. The more grooves, the smaller the cord you will need to use. An example is a seven-groove foot with #3 perle cotton. Experiment and make notes of what you need to do to get great results.*

3. Leave about 1" of cord extended beyond the end of the fabric strip. Position the cord and the fabric under the foot, making sure that the cord is securely in the groove.

4. Holding the seam allowances on the right of the foot, straight stitch along the cord.

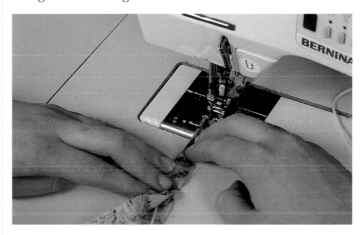

Always make the piping strip longer than you need so that you do not have to worry about neatness or stitching into the cord at the beginning. Once the length is stitched, trim the seam allowance to $1/4$", but do not pull out the cord.

When attaching the piping to the block, use the same piping foot you used to make the stem. Position and stitch as instructed in Method #4. Once it is stitched in place, cut to length and pull out the cord. Trim the excess seam allowance to a scant $1/8$" or smaller if needed. Bend the strip over the seam allowance and Invisible Machine appliqué (Chapter Fifteen) the folded edge in place. If the ends need to be finished, refer to the following section.

Finishing the Ends of Bias Strips

There are many times that a stem is not under anything else, requiring one or both ends to be finished. To do this easily, determine the length needed for each stem, then add a minimum of 1" to that measurement. Cut. On one end, open the seam allowances of the bias. Turn the raw end in about 1/4". Press. Reposition the seam allowances and press. Repeat for the other end if needed, re-measuring and trimming to get exactly the right length when finished.

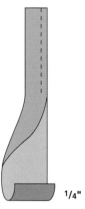

1/4"

Using Photocopy Machines

I have saved hundreds of hours in preparation time by experimenting with copy machines. These wonderful tools can be a quilter's best friend, next to the sewing machine and the computer!

Find a copier that you can play with. We will be doing some unorthodox things with it, so it is best to have your own or use a friend's. Perhaps you know someone who has one in an office you can have access to. Don't be totally put off by purchasing one. The size you need is the desktop size, not a large, high-speed copier, and it should be able to enlarge and reduce. How many times have you needed a pattern or quilting design just slightly larger or smaller? The copier also needs to have a manual feed system, as we will not be able to use the paper tray feed system for these techniques. Reduction and enlargement features are extremely valuable to a quilter.

The following ideas are just a start. Experiment, and see what shortcuts the copier can do for you. So far, I have never jammed or harmed a machine with the ideas presented here. Just go slowly at first, and don't try to force the copier to do anything it doesn't readily accept.

Pattern-Making Tips Using the Photocopier

COPYING PATTERNS DIRECTLY ONTO FREEZER PAPER

The most timesaving use of the copier is pattern reproductions. How many hours have you spent sitting and tracing the same design element over and over? And how accurate are you able to keep the pattern after tracing it that many times? Consider letting the copier do the reproductions for you, accurately and fast. If you are working with paper patterns to be used as templates, you can make copies normally. However, if you are hooked on freezer paper, the copier will print onto it, too! Here's how:

❂ Cut the freezer paper to the exact size of a sheet of copier paper.

❂ Place the master pattern on the top of the machine. Place the freezer paper, plastic coated side down, on top of a sheet of copier paper.

🖤 NOTE: If you run freezer paper through the machine by itself, the heat of the machine will alter the adhesion properties of the plastic.

❂ Using the manual feed slot, slowly insert the two papers. The feeding rollers will pick up both and feed them through evenly. The master pattern will be printed onto the freezer paper.

❂ Gently pull the two papers apart. (They will stick together slightly, but this does not affect the freezer paper's ability to stick to the fabric.)

Think of what a time saver this will be when you're tracing hundreds of pie-shaped pieces for Drunkard's Path or Clamshells or making the same appliqué block twenty-five times for a full-size quilt.

MAKING COPIES FOR A PATTERN LAYOUT

Many patterns come as a half or quarter of the design. This is necessary because of paper size limitation for books and patterns.

You can make two or four copies of the original and tape them together to have the complete pattern to use when laying out the appliqué pieces.

PHOTOCOPYING DIRECTLY ONTO FABRIC

Believe it or not, you can run fabric through the copier and achieve a screen-printed effect with the toner. First, the size of the project is limited to one thickness of fabric, at least one inch smaller on all sides than a sheet of copier paper.

1. Secure the fabric to the paper with Scotch® Magic™ Tape. Use only this brand of tape because cellophane tapes melt in the machine. Tape around the edges of the fabric.

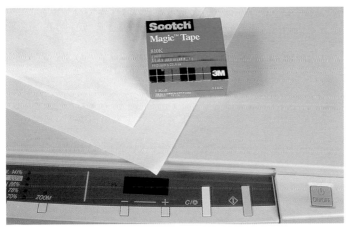

2. Place the master design you wish to copy on the top of the machine. Slowly insert the fabric/paper sheet into the manual feed slot.

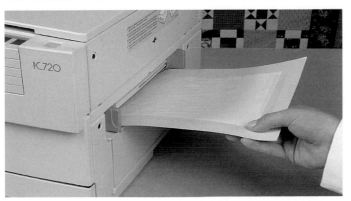

3. When it appears on the other side, the master design is transferred onto the fabric, an exact duplicate. Heat-set the toner into the fabric with a pressing cloth and hot iron.

June Taylor™ now has colorfast fabric available for copying images onto fabric with an inkjet machine. Color copies are colorfast to washing without any special treatment. There are numerous other products available that will allow you to transfer images onto fabric using a laser or inkjet printer or copier. Check with your local quilt shop for more information about the products available.

Think of the possibilities you have now! Consider making:

▓ Labels for the backs of your quilts—possibly from a business card or other original design.

▓ Care labels for your products.

▓ Or use any of the numerous label design books to reproduce designs directly onto muslin instead of tracing them.

Photocopying Fabric for Designing

I was first introduced to this idea by Jinny Beyer in a color class she was teaching. She passed out stacks of "paper fabric" that had been made by photocopying her designer fabrics. As we worked with the papers, the importance of value to quilt designing became apparent.

Fabric can be placed directly onto the top of a copy machine and "photographed." The result is a gray reproduction of the print. The value is picked up through the gray and is comparable to working with a gray scale. This is often useful in planning scrap quilts, where the value of the fabric is as important, if not more so, than the actual color. Each fabric will photocopy differently, based on its value.

By copying many different fabrics of various print scales, pattern repeats, values, etc., you can design quilts without regard to color.

Photocopiers Used for Enlarging and Reducing

Copy machines are invaluable for enlarging and reducing patterns. Thanks to them, long gone are the days of using graph paper and charting out the size differences. Below is a handy chart to determine the percentage at which to set the machine to get a new size pattern. You can also find enlargement/reduction scales at office supply stores.

Enlarging & Reducing Photocopy Chart	1"	2"	3"	4"	5"	6"	7"	8"	9"
1"	100%	200%	300%	400%	500%	600%	700%	800%	900%
2"	50%	100%	150%	200%	250%	300%	350%	400%	450%
3"	33%	66%	100%	133%	166%	200%	233%	266%	300%
4"	25%	50%	75%	100%	125%	150%	175%	200%	225%
5"	20%	40%	60%	80%	100%	120%	140%	160%	180%
6"	17%	33%	50%	67%	83%	100%	117%	133%	150%
7"	14%	28%	43%	52%	71%	86%	100%	114%	128%
8"	12%	25%	37%	50%	62%	75%	87%	100%	112%
9"	11%	22%	33%	44%	55%	66%	77%	88%	100%

To use the chart to enlarge a 3" pattern to a 6" pattern, look across from the left column (3") and down from the top row (6"). The percentage is 200%. To reduce 8" to 5", look down to 8" and across to 5". It is 62%. 100% refers to same size. 4" to 4$^{1}/_{2}$" would be halfway between 4" (100%) and 5" (125%) or 112% on a copy machine.

Gallery

Currants and Coxcomb by Harriet Hargrave. Satin stitched, machine quilted. 42" x 42"

Tulips by the Path
by Harriet Hargrave.
From a pattern from The Stitch
Connection. Appliqué techniques
used to create the appliqué and
curved pieces made it possible to
complete the top in seven hours.
Machine quilted. 42" x 42"

Oriental Poppy
Buttonhole stitch appliqué by Nancy
Hieronymus Barret, quilted by
Harriet Hargrave. Adapted from an
1871 quilt pattern and a 1937 quilt
made by Charlotte Jane Whitehill.
Machine quilted. 82" x 82"

Ohio Rose
by Harriet Hargrave.
Invisible Machine appliqué
techniques were used to
reproduce this 1930s classic.
Machine quilted. 62" x 62"

California Rose
by Sharyn Craig.
Straight stitch appliqué
 technique. Hand quilted.
62" x 62"

Sadiei's Choice
by Harriet Hargrave.
Late 1800s pattern using
Invisible Machine appliqué
techniques. Machine quilted.
50" x 50"

Calico Garden
by Harriet Hargrave.
Combination of Invisible and
Buttonhole stitch appliqué techniques.
Pattern from Debra Wagner, adapted
from a 1951 design by Florence Peto.
Machine quilted. 33" x 33"

Baltimore Friendship Quilt
by Barbara Alpan, Springfield, IL
using Blanket stitch appliqué techniques.
Machine quilted 70" x 70"

Coventry Stars
by Harriet Hargrave.
Pattern by Jo Morton of Prairie
Hands Patterns, adapted from a
quilt c.1830-1850. Invisible
Machine appliqué technique used.
Machine quilted. 51" x 51"

Christmas Lily
by Harriet Hargrave.
Adapted from a Christmas card,
this quilt uses Straight stitch
appliqué for the leaves and stems,
stenciling for the sashing strips.
Machine quilted. 70" x 70"

Drunkard's Path
by Harriet Hargrave.
Curved piecing was
eliminated by using the curved
piecing à la appliqué technique.
Machine quilted. 52" x 52"

Baltimore Garden
Invisible machine appliquéd
by Barbara Trumbo,
Machine quilted by Harriet
Hargrave. 62" x 62"

Variable Star and Nine Patch
by Harriet and Carrie Hargrave.
This quilt is a close replication of a c.
1800 central medallion quilt. Harriet's
daughter Carrie designed the *broderie
perse* center; Harriet Buttonhole stitched
the edges. Machine quilted. 63" x 76"

Irish Rose
Late 1800s antique quilt from
the collection of the author.
Straight stitch appliqué with
white thread. Hand quilted.
76" x 84"

The Rose
by Cathy Robiscoe.
Cathy's method of reverse appliqué
achieves a detailed leaded glass
piece without using bias tape.
Original design by Cathy.

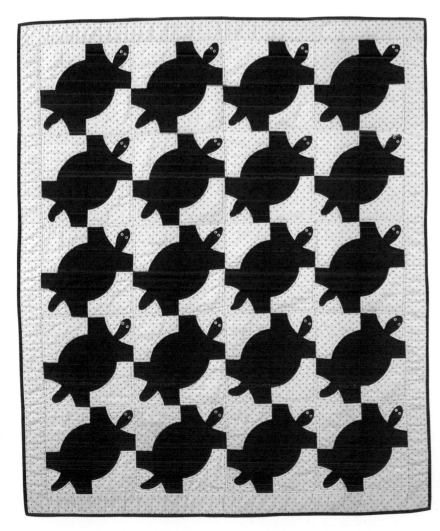

Turtle Quilt
by Harriet Hargrave.
Adapted from a late 19th century quilt by an
unknown African-American quilt-maker. Harriet
was commissioned to make this quilt for the
movie *Switchback*. She made three of them for
the production company in 10 days using the
curved piecing à la appliqué technique in
Chapter 16. Machine quilted. 38" x 46"

Zia
by Gail Garber. Gail used machine
stained glass techniques to create
this New Mexico sun symbol.

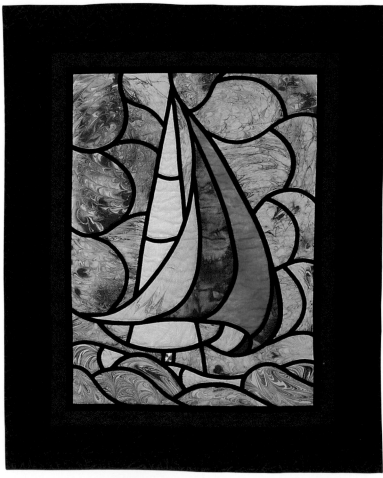

Catamaran
by Mace McEligot.
This is an original design using her
own hand-dyed and marbelized
fabrics. Mace stitched the bias
using the blanket stitch.

Practice Patterns

Practice Patterns

5

6

8

3

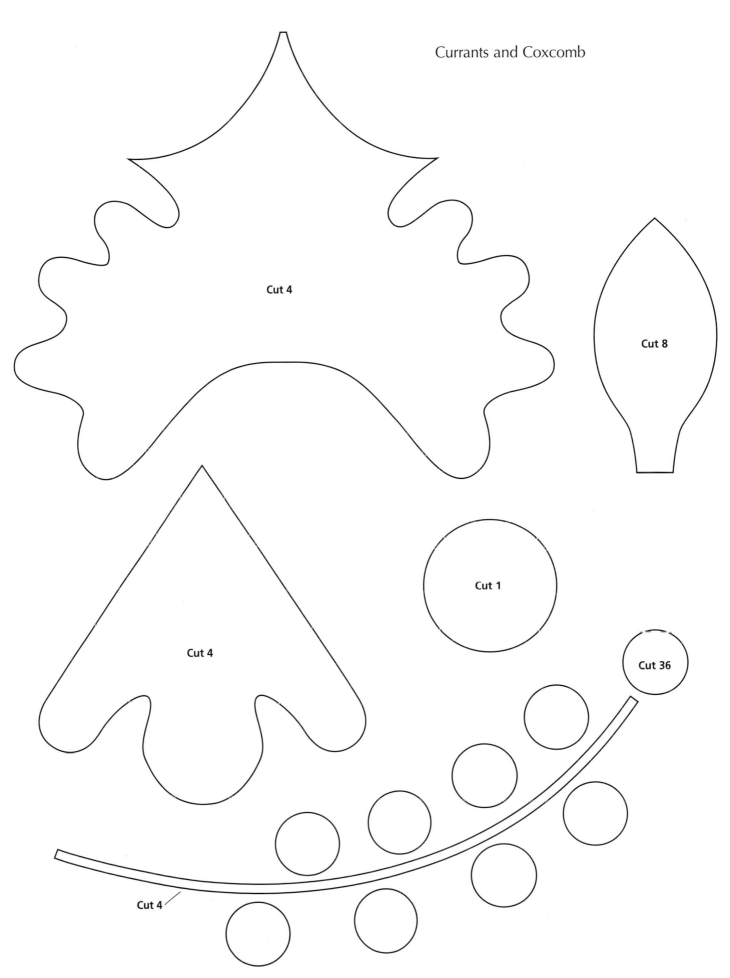

Currants and Coxcomb

Cut 4

Cut 8

Cut 4

Cut 1

Cut 36

Cut 4

Currants and Coxcomb

Enlarge 200%

Ohio Rose

Cut 4

Cut 4

Cut 4

Cut 4

Cut 4

Cut 4

Center

Index

For more information write
for a free catalog:
C&T Publishing, Inc.
P.O. Box 1456
Lafayette, CA 94549
(800) 284-1114
e-mail: ctinfo@ctpub.com
website: www.ctpub.com

For quilting supplies:

Harriet's Treadle Arts
6390 West 44th Avenue
Wheat Ridge, CO 80033
(303) 424-2742
(303) 424-1290 fax
e-mail: Harriet@hjh@ecentral.com
website: www.harriethargrave.com

Cotton Patch Mail Order
3405 Hall Lane, Dept. CTB
Lafayette, CA 94549
(800) 835-4418
(925) 283-7883
e-mail: quiltusa@yahoo.com
website: www.quiltusa.com

Other Fine Books From C&T Publishing:

Along the Garden Path: More Quilters and Their Gardens, Jean Wells and Valori Wells
An Amish Adventure: 2nd Ed., Roberta Horton
The Best of Baltimore Beauties, Elly Sienkiewicz
Block Magic: Over 50 Fun & Easy Blocks made from Squares and Rectangles, Nancy Johnson-Srebro
Crazy Quilt Handbook, Revised 2nd Ed., Judith Baker Montano
Diane Phalen Quilts: 10 Projects to Celebrate the Seasons, Diane Phalen
Easy Pieces: Creative Color Play with Two Simple Blocks, Margaret Miller
Endless Possibilities: Using NO-FAIL Methods, Nancy Johnson-Srebro
Fantastic Fabric Folding: Innovative Quilting Projects, Rebecca Wat
Flower Pounding: Quilt Projects for All Ages, Amy Sandrin & Ann Frischkorn
Free Stuff for Quilters on the Internet, 3rd Ed. Judy Heim and Gloria Hansen
Free Stuff for Sewing Fanatics on the Internet, Judy Heim and Gloria Hansen
Free Stuff for Traveling Quilters on the Internet, Gloria Hansen
Free-Style Quilts: A "No Rules" Approach, Susan Carlson
Hand Appliqué with Alex Anderson: Seven Projects for Hand Appliqué, Alex Anderson
Hand Quilting with Alex Anderson: Six Projects for Hand Quilters, Alex Anderson
Heirloom Machine Quilting, Third Ed., Harriet Hargrave
Laurel Burch Quilts: Kindred Creatures, Laurel Burch
Lone Star Quilts and Beyond: Projects and Inspiration, Jan Krentz
Machine Embroidery and More: Ten Step-by-Step Projects Using Border Fabrics & Beads, Kristen Dibbs
Magical Four-Patch and Nine-Patch Quilts, Yvonne Porcella
Mastering Quilt Marking, Pepper Cory
Measure the Possibilities with Omnigrid, Nancy Johnson-Srebro
Patchwork Persuasion: Fascinating Quilts from Traditional Designs, Joen Wolfrom
The Photo Transfer Handbook: Snap It, Print It, Stitch It!, Jean Ray Laury
Piecing: Expanding the Basics, Ruth B. McDowell
Plaids & Stripes: The Use of Directional Fabrics in Quilts, Roberta Horton
Quilt Lovers' Favorites, American Patchwork & Quilting
Quilted Memories: Celebrations of Life, Mary Lou Weidman
Quilting Back to Front: Fun & Easy No-Mark Techniques, Larraine Scouler
Quilting with Carol Armstrong: 30 Quilting Patterns, Appliqué Designs, 16 Projects, Carol Armstrong
Quilts for Guys: 15 Fun Projects For Your Favorite Fella
Quilts, Quilts, and More Quilts! Diana McClun and Laura Nownes
Rotary Cutting with Alex Anderson: Tips, Techniques, and Projects, Alex Anderson
Rx for Quilters: Stitcher-Friendly Advice for Every Body, Susan Delaney Mech, M.D.
Say It with Quilts: Diana McClun and Laura Nownes
Scrap Quilts: The Art of Making Do, Roberta Horton
Setting Solutions, Sharyn Craig
Shadow Redwork with Alex Anderson: 24 Designs to Mix and Match, Alex Anderson
Simply Stars: Quilts that Sparkle, Alex Anderson
Skydyes: A Visual Guide to Fabric Painting, Mickey Lawler
Start Quilting with Alex Anderson, 2nd Ed.: Six Projects for First-Time Quilters, Alex Anderson
Stitch 'n Flip Quilts: 14 Fantastic Projects, Valori Wells
Strips 'n Curves: A New Spin on Strip Piecing, Louisa Smith
A Thimbleberries Housewarming: 22 Projects for Quilters, Lynette Jensen
Through the Garden Gate: Quilters and Their Gardens, Jean and Valori Wells
Wildflowers: Designs for Appliqué & Quilting, Carol Armstrong

About the Author

Harriet Hargrave is a well-known author, teacher, quilt shop owner, and innovator of machine quilting. She is internationally recognized for her contributions to the quilt world. She was selected in 1995 by Nihon Vogue and her peers as one of the "88 Leaders of the Quilt World." Her books, *Heirloom Machine Quilting, Mastering Machine Applique, From Fiber to Fabric* and *The Art Of Classic Quiltmaking* continue to enlighten quilt-makers around the world.

Harriet has a degree in Textiles and Clothing from Colorado State University. She is continues to be involved in developing quality quilt battings with Hobbs Bonded Fibers and designing authentic and accurate reproduction fabrics from the 19th century with P & B Textiles. She has owned and operated her quilt shop, Harriet's Treadle Arts, since 1980 in Wheat Ridge, Colorado. She resides in Arvada, Colorado.

Other Fine Books From Harriet Hargrave:

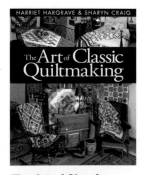

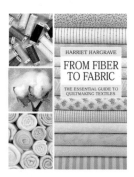

An American Quilt Retailer Classics Award winner
—Best Instructional Book for Machine Quilting

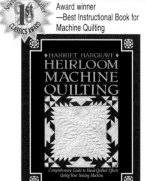

The Art of Classic Quiltmaking
by Harriet Hargrave and Sharyn Craig

From Fiber to Fabric
The Essential Guide to Quiltmaking Textiles
by Harriet Hargrave

Heirloom Machine Quilting
A Comprehensive Guide to Hand Quilted Effects Using Your Sewing Machine, Third Edition
by Harriet Hargrave

Quick-Look Guide: Choosing Batting
Take this handy guide with you to shop for batting! Filled with valuable tips and charts in an easy-to-use format.
by Harriet Hargrave

Quick-Look Guide: Caring for Fabric & Quilts
Keep this handy guide near your laundry area! Packed with valuable tips and charts in an easy-to-use format.
by Harriet Hargrave